REVELATION

Chapters 14—22

J. Vernon McGee

THOMAS NELSON PUBLISHERS

Nashville • Atlanta • London • Vancouver

Published in Nashville, Tennessee, by Thomas Nelson, Inc.

Scripture quotations are from the KING JAMES VERSION of the Bible.

Library of Congress Cataloging-in-Publication Data

McGee, J. Vernon (John Vernon), 1904–1988
     [Thru the Bible with J. Vernon McGee]
     Thru the Bible commentary series / J. Vernon McGee.
        p.   cm.
     Reprint. Originally published: Thru the Bible with J. Vernon
McGee. 1975.
     Includes bibliographical references.
     ISBN 0-7852-1066-0 (TR)
     ISBN 0-7852-1123-3 (NRM)
     1. Bible—Commentaries. I. Title.
BS491.2.M37   1991
220.7'7—dc20   90–41340
                                                          CIP

Printed in the United States of America
5 6 7 8 9 — 99 98 97 96

CONTENTS

REVELATION—Chapters 14—22

PREFACE

The radio broadcasts of the Thru the Bible Radio five-year program were transcribed, edited, and published first in single-volume paperbacks to accommodate the radio audience.

There has been a minimal amount of further editing for this publication. Therefore, these messages are not the word-for-word recording of the taped messages which went out over the air. The changes were necessary to accommodate a reading audience rather than a listening audience.

These are popular messages, prepared originally for a radio audience. They should not be considered a commentary on the entire Bible in any sense of that term. These messages are devoid of any attempt to present a theological or technical commentary on the Bible. Behind these messages is a great deal of research and study in order to interpret the Bible from a popular rather than from a scholarly (and too-often boring) viewpoint.

We have definitely and deliberately attempted "to put the cookies on the bottom shelf so that the kiddies could get them."

The fact that these messages have been translated into many languages for radio broadcasting and have been received with enthusiasm reveals the need for a simple teaching of the whole Bible for the masses of the world.

I am indebted to many people and to many sources for bringing this volume into existence. I should express my especial thanks to my secretary, Gertrude Cutler, who supervised the editorial work; to Dr. Elliott R. Cole, my associate, who handled all the detailed work with the publishers; and finally, to my wife Ruth for tenaciously encouraging me from the beginning to put my notes and messages into printed form.

Solomon wrote, ". . . of making many books there is no end; and much study is a weariness of the flesh" (Eccl. 12:12). On a sea of books that flood the marketplace, we launch this series of THRU THE BIBLE with the hope that it might draw many to the one Book, *The Bible*.

J. VERNON McGEE

REVELATION

INTRODUCTION

As we begin this book of Revelation, I have mingled feelings. I am actually running scared as we come to this, one of the great books in the Word of God. Candidly, I must also say that it is with great joy that I begin it. Let me explain why I say this.

It has long been my practice, when I need a time of relaxation, to read a mystery story, a detective story. I confess that mystery stories have been more or less a hobby of mine over the years.

I do not read much of Agatha Christie anymore for the very simple reason that I have read so many of hers that I can usually figure out who the killer is, who committed the murder. Now I read Dorothy Sayers. By the way, she is a Christian, and she gets a great deal of Scripture into her books. The unsaved are reading the Bible without realizing it. Anyway, I have always enjoyed mystery stories.

When I began my ministry, I was a single man, and on Sunday nights after the evening service, I would get into bed and read one of the mystery stories.

Well, about one o'clock in the morning I would get to the place where the heroine has been tied down to the railroad tracks by the villain, and old Number 77 is going to be coming along in about twenty minutes. She is in a desperate situation. I think that the hero is going to be able to get there and rescue her, but I find out that he is in that old warehouse down by the pier, tied to a chair under which is a stick of dynamite with the fuse already lighted! Well, I can't leave the hero and heroine at one o'clock in the morning in that kind of position. But, since it is time for me to turn over and go to sleep, I slip over to the final page. A different scene greets me there. I see the hero and the heroine sitting out in a yard. I see a lovely cottage encircled by a white picket fence. They are married now and have a little baby who is playing there on the lawn. What a wonderful, comfortable scene that is!

So I would just turn back to the place where I stopped reading, and I would say to the hero and heroine, "I don't know how you are going to get out of it, but I tell you this: It's going to work out all right."

My friend, I have a book in the Bible called the Book of the Revelation, and it tells me how this world scene is going to end. I will be frank to say that I get a little disturbed today when I see what is happening in the world. It is a dark picture as I look out at it, and I wonder how it is going to work out. Well, all I do is turn to the last book of the Bible, and when I begin to read there, I find that it's going to work out all right. Do you know that? Emerson said that *things* are in the saddle, and they ride mankind. It does look that way. In fact, it looks as if the Devil is having a high holiday in the world, and I think he is, but God is going to work it out. God Himself will gain control—in fact, He has never lost control—and He is moving to the time when He is going to place His Son, the Lord Jesus Christ, upon the throne of His universe down here. It does look dark now. I think that any person today who looks at the world situation and takes an optimistic view of it has something wrong with his thinking. The world is in a desperate condition. However, I'm no pessimist because I have the Book of Revelation, and I can say to every person who has trusted Christ, "Don't you worry. It's going to work out all right." My friend, the thing is going to come out with God on top. Therefore, I want to be with Him. As Calvin put it, "I would rather lose now and win later than to win now and lose later." I want to say to you, friend, that I am on the side that appears to be losing now, but we are going to win later. The reason I know this is because I have been reading the Book of Revelation. And I hope that you are going to read it with me.

As I have said, I approach the Book of Revelation with fear and trembling, not primarily because of a lack of competence on my part (although that may be self-evident), but many other factors enter into this feeling. First of all, there may be a lack of knowledge on the part of the readers. You see, the Book of Revelation is the sixty-sixth book of the Bible, and it comes last. This means that we need to know sixty-five other books before we get to this place. You need to have the background of a working knowledge of all the Bible that precedes it. You need to have a feel of the Scriptures as well as have the facts of the Scriptures in your mind.

There is a second factor that gives me a feeling of alarm as I enter this book. It is the contemporary climate into which we are giving these studies in Revelation. It is not primarily because of a skeptical and doubting age—although it is certainly that—but it is because of these dark and difficult and desperate days in which we live. We see the failure of leadership in every field—government, politics, science, education, military, and entertainment. Since the educators cannot control even their own campuses, how are they going to supply leadership for the world? Business is managed by tycoons. And the actors can be heard on the media talk programs. Listening to them for only a brief time reveals that they have nothing to say. They do a lot of talking, but they say nothing that is worthwhile. None of these groups or segments of our society have any solutions. They are failures in the realm of leadership. There is a glaring lack of leadership. There is no one to lead us out of this moral morass or out of the difficult and Laocoön-like problems which have us all tangled up. We are living in a very difficult time, my friend. In fact, I think that it is one of the worst in the history of the church.

Knowledgeable men have been saying some very interesting things about this present hour. Please note that I am not quoting from any preachers but from outstanding men in other walks of life.

Dr. Urey, from the University of Chicago, who worked on the atomic bomb, began an article several years ago in *Collier's* magazine by saying, "I am a frightened man, and I want to frighten you."

Dr. John R. Mott returned from a trip around the world and made the statement that this was "the most dangerous era the world has ever known." And he raised the question of where we are heading. Then he made this further statement, "When I think of human tragedy, as I saw it and felt it, of the Christian ideals sacrificed as they have been, the thought comes to me that *God is preparing the way for some immense direct action.*"

Chancellor Robert M. Hutchins, of the University of Chicago, gave many people a shock several years ago when he made the statement that "devoting our educational efforts to infants between six and twenty-one seems futile." And he added, "The world may not last long enough." He contended that for this reason we should begin adult education.

Winston Churchill said, "Time may be short."

Mr. Luce, the owner of *Life, Time,* and *Fortune* magazines, addressed a group of missionaries who were the first to return to their fields after the war. Speaking in San Francisco, he made the statement that when he was a boy, the son of a Presbyterian missionary in China, he and his father often discussed the premillennial coming of Christ, and he thought that all missionaries who believed in that teaching were inclined to be fanatical. And then Mr. Luce said, "I wonder if there wasn't something to that position after all."

It is very interesting to note that *The Christian Century* carried an article by Wesner Fallaw which said, "A function of the Christian is to make preparation for world's end."

Dr. Charles Beard, the American historian, said, "All over the world the thinkers and searchers who scan the horizon of the future are attempting to assess the values of civilization and speculating about its destiny."

Dr. William Yogt, in the *Road to Civilization,* wrote: "The handwriting on the wall of five continents now tells us that the Day of Judgment is at hand."

Dr. Raymond B. Fosdick, president of the Rockefeller Foundation, said, "To many ears comes the sound of the trump of doom. Time is short."

H. G. Wells declared before he died, "This world is at the end of its tether. The end of everything we call life is close at hand."

General Douglas MacArthur said, "We have had our last chance."

Former president Dwight Eisenhower said, "Without a moral regeneration throughout the world there is no hope for us as we are going to disappear one day in the dust of an atomic explosion."

Dr. Nicholas Murray Butler, ex-president of Columbia University, said, "The end cannot be far distant."

To make the picture even more bleak, the modern church has no solutions for the problems of this hour in which we are living. There was a phenomenal growth in church membership, especially after World War II, but that took place for only a few years. The growth went from 20 percent of the population in 1884 to 35 percent of the population in 1959. That was the high point of Protestant church membership. And it would indicate the possibility of a church on fire for God. Then it had wealth and was building tremendous programs, but recently the church has begun to lose, and it certainly is not affecting the contemporary culture of the present hour.

As far back as 1958 the late David Lawrence wrote an editorial which he entitled "The 'Mess' in the World." He described it very accurately, but even he did not have a solution for it. As we look out at the world in this present hour, we see that it is really in a *mess*.

For a long time now men in high positions have looked into the future and have said that there is a great crisis coming. (I wonder what they would say if they lived in our day!) As a result of this foreboding, there has been a growing interest in the Book of Revelation.

Although good expositors differ on the details of the Book of Revelation, when it comes to the broad interpretation, there are four major systems. (Broadus lists seven theories of interpretation and Tregelles lists three.)

1. The *preterist* interpretation is that all of Revelation has been fulfilled in the past. It had to do with local references in John's day and with the days of either Nero or Domitian. This view was held by Renan and by most German scholars, also by Elliott. The purpose of the Book of Revelation was to bring comfort to the persecuted church and was written in symbols that the Christians of that period would understand.

Now let me say that it was for the comfort of God's people, and it has been that for all ages, but to hold the preterist interpretation means that you might as well take the Book of Revelation out of the Bible, as it has no meaning at all for the present hour. This viewpoint has been answered and, I think, relegated to the limbo of lost things.

2. The *historical* interpretation is that the fulfillment of Revelation is going on continuously in the history of the church, from John's day

to the present time. Well, I believe that there is a certain amount of truth in this as far as the seven churches are concerned, as we shall see, but beyond that, it is obvious that the Book of Revelation is prophetic.

3. The *historical-spiritualist* interpretation is a refinement of the historical theory and was advanced first by Sir William Ramsay. This theory states that the two beasts are imperial and provincial Rome and that the point of the book is to encourage Christians. According to this theory, Revelation has been largely fulfilled and contains only spiritual lessons for the church today.

The system we know today as amillennialism has, for the most part, adopted this view. It dissipates and defeats the purpose of the book. In the seminary of my denomination, I studied Revelation in both Greek and English from the standpoint of the amillennialist. It was amazing to see how the facts of the Revelation could be dissipated into thin air by just saying, "Well, these are symbols." But they never were able to tell us exactly what they were symbols *of*. That was their problem. The fact of the matter is that some very unusual interpretations arise from this viewpoint. One interpreter sees Luther and the Reformation in a symbol that to another student pictures the invention of the printing press! In my opinion, interpretations of this type have hurt and defeated the purpose of the Book of Revelation.

4. The *futurist* interpretation is the view which is held by all premillennialists and is the one which I accept and present to you. It sees the Book of Revelation as primarily prophetic. Most premillennialists follow a certain form of interpretation that conforms to the Book of Revelation. (We will see this in the outline of the book.) It begins with the revelation of the glorified Christ. Then the church is brought before us, and the whole history of the church is given. Then, at the end of chapter 3, the church goes to heaven and we see it, not as the church anymore, but as the bride which will come to the earth with Christ when He comes to establish His Kingdom—that thousand-year reign that John will tell us about. It will be a time of testing, for at the end of that period Satan will be released for a brief season. Then the final rebellion is put down and eternity begins. This is the viewpoint of Revelation which is generally accepted.

In our day there are many critics of this interpretation who not only attempt to discount it but say rather harsh things about it. One recent book of criticism, written by a layman, quotes me as being unable to answer his argument. Well, the fact of the matter is that he called me at home one morning as I was getting ready to go to my office. I wasn't well at the time, and I didn't want to get involved in an argument with a man who obviously was very fanatical in his position. In his book he makes the statement that I was *unable* to answer his question. If he misquotes the other Bible expositors as he misquotes me, I would have no confidence in his book whatsoever.

In his book he maintains that the premillennial futurist viewpoint is something that is brand new. I'll admit that it has been fully developed, as have all these other interpretations, during the past few years. When I was a young man and a new Christian, I was introduced to the theory known as postmillennialism. The postmillennialists believed that the world would get better and better, that the church would convert the whole world, and then Christ would come and reign. Well, that viewpoint is almost dead today. After two world wars, a worldwide depression, and the crises through which the world is passing, there are very few who still hold that viewpoint. By the time I enrolled in the seminary of my denomination, every professor was an amillennialist, that is, they didn't believe in a Millennium. It was to that view that most of the postmillennialists ran for cover. There was one professor in the seminary who was still a postmillennialist. He was very old and hard of hearing. In fact, when they told him that the war was over, he thought they meant the Civil War. He was really a back number, and he was still a postmillennialist.

At the risk of being a little tedious, I am going to give you the viewpoints of many men in the past to demonstrate that they were looking for Christ to return. They were not looking for the Great Tribulation, they were not even looking for the Millennium, but they were looking for Him to come. This expectation is the very heart of the premillennial viewpoint as we hold it today.

Barnabas, who was a co-worker with the apostle Paul, has been quoted as saying, "The true Sabbath is the one thousand years . . . when Christ comes back to reign."

xiv   INTRODUCTION

Clement (A.D. 96), Bishop of Rome, said, "Let us every hour expect the kingdom of God . . . we know not the day."

Polycarp (A.D. 108), Bishop of Smyrna and finally burned at the stake there, said, "He will raise us from the dead . . . we shall . . . reign with Him."

Ignatius, Bishop of Antioch, who the historian Eusebius says was the apostle Peter's successor, commented, "Consider the times and expect Him."

Papias (A.D. 116), Bishop of Hierapolis, who—according to Irenaeus—saw and heard the apostle John, said, "There will be one thousand years . . . when the reign of Christ personally will be established on earth."

Justin Martyr (A.D. 150) said, "I and all others who are orthodox Christians, on all points, know there will be a thousand years in Jerusalem . . . as Isaiah and Ezekiel declared."

Irenaeus (A.D. 175), Bishop of Lyons, commenting on Jesus' promise to drink again of the fruit of the vine in His Father's Kingdom, argues: "That this . . . can only be fulfilled upon our Lord's personal return to earth."

Tertullian (A.D. 200) said, "We do indeed confess that a kingdom is promised on earth."

Martin Luther said, "Let us not think that the coming of Christ is far off."

John Calvin, in his third book of *Institutes*, wrote: "Scripture uniformly enjoins us to look with expectation for the advent of Christ."

Canon A. R. Fausset said this: "The early Christian fathers, Clement, Ignatius, Justin Martyr, and Irenaeus, looked for the Lord's speedy return as the necessary precursor of the millennial kingdom. Not until the professing Church lost her first love, and became the harlot resting on the world power, did she cease to be the Bride going forth to meet the Bridegroom, and seek to reign already on earth without waiting for His Advent."

Dr. Elliott wrote: "All primitive expositors, except Origen and the few who rejected Revelation, were premillennial."

Gussler's work on church history says of this blessed hope that "it was so distinctly and prominently mentioned that we do not hesitate in regarding it as the general belief of that age."

Chillingworth declared: "It was the doctrine believed and taught by the most eminent fathers of the age next to the apostles and by none of that age condemned."

Dr. Adolf von Harnack wrote: "The earlier fathers—Irenaeus, Hippolytus, Tertullian, etc.—believed it because it was part of the tradition of the early church. It is the same all through the third and fourth centuries with those Latin theologians who escaped the influence of Greek speculation."

My friend, I have quoted these many men of the past as proof of the fact that from the days of the apostles and through the church of the first centuries the interpretation of the Scriptures was premillennial. When someone makes the statement that premillennialism is something that originated one hundred years ago with an old witch in England, he doesn't know what he is talking about. It is interesting to note that premillennialism was the belief of these very outstanding men of the early church.

There are six striking and singular features about the Book of Revelation.

1. It is the only prophetic book in the New Testament. There are seventeen prophetic books in the Old Testament and only this one in the New Testament.

2. John, the writer, reaches farther back into eternity past than does any other writer in Scripture. He does this in his Gospel which opens with this: "In the beginning was the Word, and the Word was with God, and the Word was God" (John 1:1). Then he moves up to the time of creation: "All things were made by him; and without him was not any thing made that was made" (John 1:3). Then, when John writes the Book of Revelation, he reaches farther on into eternity future and the eternal Kingdom of our Lord and Savior Jesus Christ.

3. There is a special blessing which is promised to the readers of this book: "Blessed is he that readeth, and they that hear the words of this prophecy, and keep those things which are written therein: for the time is at hand" (Rev. 1:3). It is a blessing promise. Also, there is a

warning given at the end of the book issued to those who tamper with its contents: "For I testify unto every man that heareth the words of the prophecy of this book, If any man shall add unto these things, God shall add unto him the plagues that are written in this book: and if any man shall take away from the words of the book of this prophecy, God shall take away his part out of the book of life, and out of the holy city, and from the things which are written in this book" (Rev. 22:18–19). That warning ought to make these wild and weird interpreters of prophecy stop, look, and listen. It is dangerous to say just *anything* relative to the Book of Revelation because people today realize that we have come to a great crisis in history. To say something that is entirely out of line is to mislead them. Unfortunately, the most popular prophetic teachers in our day are those who have gone out on a limb. This has raised a very serious problem, and later on we will have repercussions from it.

4. It is not a *sealed* book. Daniel was told to seal the book until the time of the end (see Dan. 12:9), but John is told: "Seal not the sayings of the prophecy of this book: for the time is at hand" (Rev. 22:10). To say that the Book of Revelation is a jumble and impossible to make heads or tails out of and cannot be understood is to contradict this. It is not a sealed book. In fact, it is probably the best organized book in the Bible.

5. It is a series of visions expressed in symbols which deal with *reality*. The literal interpretation is always preferred unless John makes it clear that it is otherwise.

6. It is like a great union station where the great trunk lines of prophecy have come in from other portions of Scripture. Revelation does not originate or begin anything. Rather it consummates and concludes that which has been begun somewhere else in Scripture. It is imperative to a right understanding of the book to be able to trace each great subject of prophecy from the first reference to the terminal. There are at least ten great subjects of prophecy which find their consummation here. This is the reason that a knowledge of the rest of the Bible is imperative to an understanding of the Book of Revelation. It is calculated that there are over five hundred references or allusions to

the Old Testament in Revelation and that, of its 404 verses, 278 contain references to the Old Testament. In other words, over half of this book depends upon your understanding of the Old Testament.

Let's look at the Book of Revelation as an airport with ten great airlines coming into it. We need to understand where each began and how it was developed as it comes into the Book of Revelation. The ten great subjects of prophecy which find their consummation here are these:

1. The Lord Jesus Christ. He is the subject of the book. The subject is not the beasts nor the bowls of wrath but the Sin-bearer. The first mention of Him is way back in Genesis 3:15, as the Seed of the woman.

2. The church does not begin in the Old Testament. It is first mentioned by the Lord Jesus in Matthew 16:18: "And I say also unto thee, That thou art Peter, and upon this rock I will build my church; and the gates of hell shall not prevail against it."

3. The resurrection and the translation of the saints (see John 14; 1 Thess. 4:13–18; 1 Cor. 15:51–52).

4. The Great Tribulation, spoken of back in Deuteronomy 4 where God says that His people would be in tribulation.

5. Satan and evil (see Ezek. 28:11–18).

6. The "man of sin" (see Ezek. 28:1–10).

7. The course and end of apostate Christendom (see Dan. 2:31–45; Matt. 13).

8. The beginning, course, and end of the "times of the Gentiles" (see Dan. 2:37–45; Luke 21:24). The Lord Jesus said that Jerusalem will be trodden down of the Gentiles until the Times of the Gentiles are fulfilled.

9. The second coming of Christ. According to Jude 14–15, Enoch spoke of that, which takes us back to the time of the Genesis record.

10. Israel's covenants, beginning with the covenant which God made with Abraham in Genesis 12:1–3. God promised Israel five things, and God says in Revelation that He will fulfill them all.

Now I want to make a positive statement: The Book of Revelation is not a difficult book. The liberal theologian has tried to make it a difficult book, and the amillennialist considers it a symbolic and hard-to-understand book. Even some of our premillennialists are trying to demonstrate that it is weird and wild.

Actually, it is the most orderly book in the Bible. And there is no reason to misunderstand it. This is what I mean: It divides itself. John puts down the instructions given to him by Christ: "Write the things which thou hast seen, and the things which are, and the things which shall be hereafter" (Rev. 1:19)—past, present, and future. Then we will find that the book further divides itself in series of sevens, and each division is as orderly as it possibly can be. You will find no other book in the Bible that divides itself like that.

To those who claim that it is all symbolic and beyond our understanding, I say that the Book of Revelation is to be taken literally. And when a symbol is used, it will be so stated. Also it will be symbolic of reality, and the reality will be more real than the symbol for the simple reason that John uses symbols to describe reality. In our study of the book, that is an all-important principle to follow. Let's allow the Revelation to say what it wants to say.

Therefore, we have no right to reach into the book and draw out of it some of the wonderful pictures that John describes for us and interpret them as taking place in our day. Some of them are symbolic, symbolic of reality, but not of a reality which is currently taking place.

The church is set before us in the figure of seven churches which were real churches in existence in John's day. I have visited the ruins of all seven of them and have spent many hours there. In fact, I have visited some of them on four occasions, and I would love to go back tomorrow. To examine the ruins and study the locality is a very wonderful experience. It has made these churches live for me, and I can see how John was speaking into local situations but also giving the history of the church as a whole.

Then after chapter 3, the church is not mentioned anymore. The church is not the subject again in the entire Book of the Revelation. You may ask, "Do you mean that the church goes out of business?" Well, it leaves the earth and goes to heaven, and there it appears as the bride of Christ. When we see her in the last part of Revelation, she is not the church but the bride.

Then beginning with chapter 4, everything is definitely in the future from our vantage point at the present time. So when anyone reaches in and pulls out a revelation—some vision about famine or wars or anything of that sort—it just does not fit into the picture of our day. We need to let John tell it like it is. In fact, we need to let the whole Bible speak to us like that—just let it say what it wants to say. The idea of making wild and weird interpretations is one of the reasons I enter this book with a feeling of fear.

It is interesting to note that the subject of prophecy is being developed in our day. The great doctrines of the church have been developed in certain historical periods. At first, it was the doctrine of the Scripture being the Word of God. This was followed by the doctrine of the person of Christ, known as Christology. Then the doctrine of soteriology, or salvation, was developed. And so it has been down through the years. Now you and I are living in a day when prophecy is really being developed, and we need to exercise care as to what and to whom we listen.

When the Pilgrims sailed for America, their pastor at Leyden reminded them, "The Lord has more truth yet to break forth from His Holy Word. . . . Luther and Calvin were great shining lights in their times, yet they penetrated not the whole counsel of God. . . . Be ready to receive whatever truth shall be made known to you from the written word of God." That, my friend, is very good advice because God is not revealing His truth by giving you a vision or a dream or a new religion. Therefore, we need to be very sure that all new truth comes from a correct interpretation of the *Word of God*.

As I have indicated, the twentieth century has witnessed a renewed interest in eschatology (the doctrine of last things) which we call prophecy. Especially since World War I, great strides have been made in this field. New light has fallen upon this phase of Scripture. All of this attention has focused the light of deeper study on the Book of Revelation.

In the notes which I have made on this book, I have attempted to avoid the pitfall of presenting something new and novel just for the sake of being different. Likewise, I have steered clear of repeating threadbare clichés. Many works on Revelation are merely carbon copies of other works. In my own library I have more commentaries on the Revelation than on any other book of the Bible, and most of them are almost copies of those that have preceded them.

Another danger we need to avoid is that of thinking that the Book of Revelation can be put on a chart. Although I myself have a chart and have used it in teaching, I will not be using it in this study. The reason is that if it includes all it should, it is so complicated that nobody will understand it. On the other hand, if it is so brief that it can be understood, it doesn't give enough information. I have several charts sent to me by different men in whom I have great confidence. One of them is so complicated that I need a chart to understand his chart! So, although I won't be using a chart, I will use the brief sketch below to attempt to simplify the different stages of the Revelation and also give the overall picture.

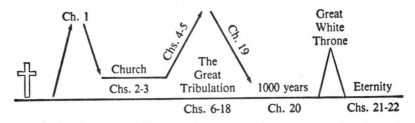

As you can see, it begins with the Cross of Christ and His ascension. In chapter 1, we see the glorified Christ. In chapters 2—3 we see the church. In chapters 4—5 we see that the church is in heaven. Then on earth the Great Tribulation takes place, chapters 6—18. In chapter 19 we see that Christ returns to the earth and establishes His Kingdom, and chapter 20 gives us the thousand-year reign of Christ. Then the Great White Throne is set up, the place where the lost are judged, and in chapters 21—22 eternity begins. That is the Book of Revelation.

Stauffer has made an important observation:

Domitian was also the first emperor to wage a proper campaign against Christ, and the church answered the attack under the leadership of Christ's last apostle, John of the Apocalypse. Nero had Paul and Peter destroyed, but he looked upon them as seditious Jews. Domitian was the first emperor to understand that behind the Christian movement there stood an enigmatic figure who threatened the glory of the emperors. He was the first to declare war on this figure, and the first also to lose the war—a foretaste of things to come.

The subject of this book is very important to see. To emphasize and reemphasize it, let me direct your attention to chapter 1, verse 1— "The Revelation of *Jesus Christ*, which God gave unto him, to shew unto his servants things which must shortly come to pass" (italics mine). Let's keep in mind that this book is a revelation of Jesus Christ. In the Gospels you see Him in the days of His flesh, but they do not give the full revelation of Jesus Christ. There you see Him in humiliation. Here in Revelation you see Him in glory. You see Him in charge of everything that takes place. He is in full command. This is the *unveiling* of Jesus Christ.

Snell has put it so well that I would like to quote him:

In the Revelation the Lamb is the center around which all else is clustered, the foundation upon which everything lasting is built, the nail on which all hangs, the object to which all points, and the spring from which all blessing proceeds. The Lamb is the light, the glory, the life, the Lord of heaven and earth, from whose face all defilement must flee away, and in whose presence fullness of joy is known. Hence we cannot go far in the study of the Revelation without seeing the Lamb. Like direction posts along the road to remind us that He, who did by Himself purge our sins, is now highly exalted and that to Him every knee must bow and every tongue confess.

To that grand statement I say hallelujah! For the Lamb is going to reign upon this earth. That is God's intention, and that is God's purpose.

As I have said, the Book of Revelation is not really a difficult book. It divides itself very easily. This is one book that doesn't require our labor in making divisions in it. John does it all for us according to the instructions given to him. In verse 18 of the first chapter the Lord Jesus speaks as the glorified Christ: "I am he that liveth, and was dead; and, behold, I am alive for evermore, Amen; and have the keys of hell and of death." Notice the four grand statements He makes concerning Himself: "I am alive. I was dead. I am alive for evermore. And I have the keys of hell [the grave] and of death." Then He tells John to write, and He gives him his outline in chapter 1, verse 19: "Write the things which thou hast seen, and the things which are, and the things which shall be hereafter." My friend, this is a wonderful, grand division that He is giving. In fact, there is nothing quite like it.

He first says, "I am he that liveth." And He instructs John, "Write the things which thou hast seen." That is past tense, referring to the vision of the Son of Man in heaven, the glorified Christ in chapter 1.

Then He says, "I was dead, and, behold, I am alive." And His instruction is, "Write the things which are." This is present tense, referring to Christ's present ministry. We are going to see that the living Christ is very busy doing things today. Do you realize that He is the Head of the church? Do you know the reason the contemporary church is in such a mess? The reason is that the church is like a body that has been decapitated. It is no longer in touch with the Head of the church. We will see Christ's ministry to the church in chapters 2—3.

Thirdly, Christ said, "I have the keys of hell and of death." And when we get to chapter 5, we will see that no one could be found to open the book but one—the Lord Jesus Christ. So chapters 4—22 deal with the future, and Christ said to John, "Write the things that you are about to see after these things." It is very important to see that "after these things" is the Greek *meta tauta*. After what things? After the church things. So in chapters 4—22 he is dealing with things that are going to take place after the church leaves the earth. The fallacy of the hour is reaching into this third section and trying to pull those events up to the present. This gives rise to the wild and weird interpretations we hear in our day. Why don't we follow what John tells us? He gives us the past, present, and future of the Book of Revelation. He will let us know when he gets to the *meta tauta*, the "after these things." You can't miss it—unless you follow a system of interpretation that doesn't fit into the Book of Revelation.

As you will see by the outline that follows, I have used the divisions which John has given to us:

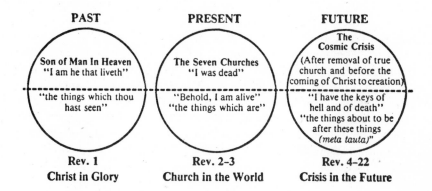

PAST	PRESENT	FUTURE
		The Cosmic Crisis
Son of Man In Heaven "I am he that liveth"	The Seven Churches "I was dead"	(After removal of true church and before the coming of Christ to creation)
"the things which thou hast seen"	"Behold, I am alive" "the things which are"	"I have the keys of hell and of death" "the things about to be after these things (meta tauta)"
Rev. 1	Rev. 2–3	Rev. 4–22
Christ in Glory	Church in the World	Crisis in the Future

   I. The Person of Jesus Christ—Christ in glory, chapter 1.
  II. The Possession of Jesus Christ—the church in the world is His, chapters 2—3.
 III. The Program of Jesus Christ—as seen in heaven, chapters 4—22.

The last section deals with the consummation of all things on this earth. This is what makes Revelation such a glorious and wonderful book.

In the first division of the Book of Revelation we will see the person of Christ in His position and glory as the Great High Priest who is in charge of His church. We will see that He is in absolute control. In the Gospels we find Him to be meek, lowly, and humble. He made Himself subject to His enemies on earth and died upon a cross! We find a completely different picture of Him in the Book of the Revelation. Here He is in absolute control. Although He is still the Lamb of God, it is His wrath that is revealed, the wrath of the Lamb, and it terrifies the earth. When He speaks in wrath, His judgment begins upon the earth.

The person of Jesus Christ is the theme of this book. When the scene moves to heaven, we see Him there, too, controlling everything. Not only in Revelation but in the entire Bible Jesus Christ is the major theme. The Scriptures are both theocentric and Christocentric, God-centered and Christ-centered. Since Christ is God, He is the One who fills the horizon of the total Word of God. This needs to be kept in mind in a special way as we study the Book of Revelation—even more than in the Gospels. The Bible as a whole tells us what He has done, what He is doing, and what He will do. The Book of Revelation emphasizes both what He *is doing* and what He *will do*.

The last book of the Old Testament, Malachi, closes with the mention of the Son of Righteousness which is yet to rise. It holds out a hope for a cursed earth, and that hope is the coming again of the Lord Jesus Christ. The Book of Revelation closes with the Bright and Morning Star, which is a figure of Christ at His coming to take the church out of the world. The Rapture is the hope of the New Testament, just as the revelation of Christ was the hope of the Old Testament. And the Book of Revelation will complete the revelation of Christ.

Notice also that there is a tie between Genesis and Revelation, the first and last books of the Bible. Genesis presents the beginning, and Revelation presents the end. Note the contrasts between the two books:

In Genesis the earth was created; in Revelation the earth passes away.

In Genesis was Satan's first rebellion; in Revelation is Satan's last rebellion.

In Genesis the sun, moon, and stars were for earth's government; in Revelation these same heavenly bodies are for earth's judgment. In Genesis the sun was to govern the day; in Revelation there is no need of the sun.

In Genesis darkness was called night; in Revelation there is "no night there" (see Rev. 21:25; 22:5).

In Genesis the waters were called seas; in Revelation there is no more sea.

In Genesis was the entrance of sin; in Revelation is the exodus of sin.

In Genesis the curse was pronounced; in Revelation the curse is removed.

In Genesis death entered; in Revelation there is no more death.

In Genesis was the beginning of sorrow and suffering; in Revelation there will be no more sorrow and no more tears.

In Genesis was the marriage of the first Adam; in Revelation is the marriage of the Last Adam.

In Genesis we saw man's city, Babylon, being built; in Revelation we see man's city, Babylon, destroyed and God's city, the New Jerusalem, brought into view.

In Genesis Satan's doom was pronounced; in Revelation Satan's doom is executed.

It is interesting that Genesis opens the Bible not only with a global view but also with a universal view—"In the beginning God created the heaven and the earth" (Gen. 1:1). And the Bible closes with another global and universal book. The Revelation shows what God is going to do with His universe and with His creatures. There is no other book quite like this.

OUTLINE

I. **The Person of Jesus Christ—Christ in Glory, Chapter 1**
   A. Title of the Book, Chapter 1:1
   B. Method of Revelation, Chapter 1:2
   C. Beatitude of Bible Study, Chapter 1:3
   D. Greetings from John the Writer and from Jesus Christ in Heaven, Chapter 1:4–8
   E. The Post-Incarnate Christ in a Glorified Body, Judging His Church (the Great High Priest in the Holy of Holies), Chapter 1:9–18
      "we know him no longer after the flesh"
   F. Time Division of the Contents of Apocalypse, Chapter 1:19
   G. Interpretation of the Seven Stars and Seven Lampstands, Chapter 1:20

II. **The Possession of Jesus Christ—The Church in the World, Chapters 2—3**
   A. Letter of Christ to the Church in Ephesus, Chapter 2:1–7
   B. Letter of Christ to the Church in Smyrna, Chapter 2:8–11
   C. Letter of Christ to the Church in Pergamum, Chapter 2:12–17
   D. Letter of Christ to the Church in Thyatira, Chapter 2:18–29
   E. Letter of Christ to the Church in Sardis, Chapter 3:1–6
   F. Letter of Christ to the Church in Philadelphia, Chapter 3:7–13
   G. Letter of Christ to the Church in Laodicea, Chapter 3:14–22

III. **The Program of Jesus Christ—The Scene in Heaven, Chapters 4—22**
   A. The Church in Heaven with Christ, Chapters 4—5
      "I will come again, and receive you unto myself; that where I am there ye may be also"
      1. Throne of God, Chapter 4:1–3
      2. Twenty-four Elders, Chapter 4:4–5

CHAPTER 14

THEME: Looking to the end of the Great Tribulation

This chapter contains several events. It is an interlude in which we see the Lamb on Mount Zion, hear the proclamation of the everlasting gospel, the pronouncement of judgment upon Babylon and on those who receive the mark of the Beast, then the praise for those who die in the Lord, and the preview of Armageddon.

The chapter before us constitutes an hiatus in the series of seven performers. It is obvious that this interlude could not be fitted in between the sixth and seventh performers who are the two wild Beasts. Of course, they had to be considered together, as they are like Siamese twins, and the continuity between them could not be broken. Therefore, this interlude follows the seventh performer in recognition of the logical sequence of this book, which is not a hodgepodge of visions but unfolds in a logical, chronological, and mathematical order.

There are certain performers called to our attention in this chapter (others beside the seven whom we have seen previously) in order to give us a full-orbed view of the spectacular events of the previous two chapters. As we have seen, this is the darkest day and the most horrible hour in the history of the world. It is truly hell's holiday. Every thoughtful mind must inevitably ask the question, "How did God's people fare during this period? Could they remain faithful to the Lord through to the end with the overwhelming odds against them?" The answer is found in this chapter before us.

The Shepherd who began with 144,000 sheep is now identified with them as the Lamb. And notice that He doesn't have 143,999 sheep; He has 144,000 sheep—He did not lose one! He redeemed them, He sealed them, and He kept them, for He is the Great Shepherd of the sheep. These sheep are of a different fold from the one we are in today, and the Good Shepherd brought them through the Great Tribulation. That is the picture before us as we open this chapter. It is encouraging to know that the Lamb—not the two Beasts—is going to have the last word. And He is not a lamb that speaks like a dragon; He is the Lord Jesus Himself. And since He is going to have the final word, Babylon will fall—the great political capital, the great commercial capital, and the great religious capital of the world during the Great Tribulation period. And the followers of the Beast will be judged.

Although many of Christ's own will become martyrs during the Tribulation, they will not lose; they will win! Again I say with Calvin that I would rather be on the side that seems to be losing today but will win finally than to be on the side that seems to be winning today but is going to lose eternally. I'm glad to be on the winning side. Christ will reward those who will be martyred for Him.

In chapter 19 we will see the Lamb returning to the earth. The morning is coming. The darkness will fade away, and the Sun of Righteousness will arise with healing in His wings.

PICTURE OF THE LAMB WITH 144,000

And I looked, and, lo, a Lamb stood on the mount Sion, and with him an hundred forty and four thousand, having his Father's name written in their foreheads [Rev. 14:1].

"I saw" indicates that John is still the spectator to these events. The reel continues to roll, and the story continues to unfold.

The "Lamb" is the Lord Jesus Christ, as we have seen in chapters 5—7 and 12—13.

"Mount Sion" is at Jerusalem. There is no use trying to locate this at any other place than at Jerusalem in the land of Israel.

This verse pictures a placid, pastoral scene which opens the millennial Kingdom here upon this earth. The Lord Jesus is going to reign from Jerusalem. God Himself called it the city of the great King. And in Psalm 2:6 He says this: "Yet have I set my king upon my holy hill of Zion." It is the Father's intention to place the Lord Jesus upon the throne of David in Jerusalem, and specifically at Mount Sion.

"An hundred forty and four thousand" I believe to be the ones who were sealed back in chapter 7, although I recognize that there are some problems connected with this view. They came through the Great Tribulation like the three Hebrew children came through the fiery furnace.

Notice that the Lamb is standing with them on Mount Sion. Although He is in His person the Lamb, He is also the Shepherd. Remember that He started out with 144,000 and that He came through the Great Tribulation with 144,000. He didn't lose one.

My friend, in our day when the pressures of Satan bear us down, the living, victorious Christ is available to us. Oh, that you and I might come to know Him better and that He might occupy a greater place in our lives day by day. I am convinced in my own experience that the Lord Jesus Christ in person is the answer. When I see plaques with the motto: "Jesus is the Answer," I always say that it depends on what the question is. But certainly He is the answer to problems for which men are trying to work out solutions by some little method. They will tell you that if you follow their little legal system, you can solve the problems of your personal life, your home, your work, and your church. I doubt that there ever was a day in which there was so much teaching in all of these areas, and yet there is less victorious living in the daily experience of believers. What is the real problem today? We don't need a method; we need Christ. We need to know Him in a meaningful way. We need to draw closer to Him. By the way, when was the last time that you told Him that you loved Him? He has said that He loves you, and you ought to tell Him that in return.

> **And I heard a voice from heaven, as the voice of many waters, and as the voice of a great thunder: and I heard the voice of harpers harping with their harps:**
>
> **And they sung as it were a new song before the throne, and before the four beasts, and the elders: and no man could learn that song but the hundred and forty and four thousand, which were redeemed from the earth [Rev. 14:2–3].**

"I heard." John is not only a spectator but is also an auditor to this scene.

The 144,000 join the heavenly chorus in the Millennium. My friend, have you ever heard a choir of 144,000 voices? Well, up to this time earth has been out of tune with heaven, but here the rule of Satan is over, and the earth and heaven are in tune. What Browning said about God's being in His heaven and all's right with the world is going to be true when we get to the Millennium. All's wrong with the world right now, but in that day all will be right. The 144,000 learn the new song and join the harmony of heaven.

"I heard the voice of harpers harping with their harps." God has put His harpers in heaven while the 144,000 are on earth, on Mount Sion (that is a long way from the instruments). Having been a pastor for many years, I have heard many harpers—harping about this or that, but these are a different kind of harper. The harpers I have listened to were not musical, I can assure you. But these heavenly harpers are going to make beautiful music.

"The hundred and forty and four thousand, which were redeemed from the earth" means that they have been purchased to enter the Millennium on earth. They are not taken to heaven. Remember that this is a picture of the Millennium on earth, and these will live on the earth. The unsaved are not going to live on the earth.

"And no man could learn that song but the hundred and forty and four thousand, which were redeemed from the earth." No one can sing praises to God but the redeemed. I wish that truth could be gotten over to a great many song leaders in this day in which we live. I understand their desire to hear everybody in the congregation sing, but when they have a mixed audience of saved and unsaved people, they should not ask the unsaved to sing the songs of redemption. Don't ask them to sing:

> Amazing grace! how sweet the sound,
>   That saved a wretch like me!
> I once was lost, but now am found,
>   Was blind, but now I see.
>   "Amazing Grace"
>   —John Newton

If an unsaved person sings that, you have made him a liar. Just let the redeemed sing. The psalmist wrote: "O give thanks unto the LORD, for he is good: for his mercy endureth for ever. Let the redeemed of the LORD say so, whom he hath redeemed from the hand of the enemy" (Ps. 107:1–2). My friend, no one but the redeemed are going to say God is good. This is the reason we need a say-so Christianity in our day. We need to *say* that God is good.

But in this millennial scene, heaven and earth are brought into marvelous harmony. What a contrast this is to chapter 13 where earth is in rebellion against heaven under the Beasts. Here all is tranquility under the Lamb.

> **These are they which were not defiled with women; for they are virgins. These are they which follow the Lamb whithersoever he goeth. These were redeemed from among men, being the firstfruits unto God and to the Lamb.**

> **And in their mouth was found no guile: for they are without fault before the throne of God [Rev. 14:4–5].**

> *These are they that were not defiled (besmirched) with women; for they are virgins [Gr.: parthenoi]. These are they that follow the Lamb whithersoever He goeth. These were purchased from among men, to be the firstfruits unto God and unto the Lamb. And in their mouth was found no lie: they are without blemish.*

"Were not defiled with women; for they are virgins." What does that mean? To be frank with you, it used to puzzle me. It can have a literal or spiritual meaning, and I think it includes both. The Great Tribulation is a period of unparalleled suffering. The 144,000 have been through that period. The abnormal times demanded an abnormal state. That was the reason they were unmarried. When I was a boy, I remember a young fellow who went to war during World War I. He was engaged to a girl, but he never came home. I know other boys who married right before

they left, and they fathered children that they never saw. That was war-
time. And many girls said that they wished they had not married during that time. Well, during the Tribulation period the times are going to
be so frightful that it will be wise not to get married. You may remember
that the prophet Jeremiah also lived in a critical period, the time of the
Babylonian captivity. Because of the dark days, God forbade him to
marry: "The word of the LORD came also unto me, saying, Thou shalt
not take thee a wife, neither shalt thou have sons or daughters in this
place. For thus saith the LORD concerning the sons and concerning the
daughters that are born in this place, and concerning their mothers that
bare them, and concerning their fathers that begat them in this land;
They shall die of grievous deaths; they shall not be lamented; neither
shall they be buried; but they shall be as dung upon the face of the
earth: and they shall be consumed by the sword, and by famine; and
their carcases shall be meat for the fowls of heaven, and for the beasts
of the earth" (Jer. 16:1–4).

Our Lord Jesus mentioned those who would be mothers during the
Great Tribulation: "And woe unto them that are with child, and to
them that give suck in those days!" (Matt. 24:19).

You and I are living in a day when marriage is honorable and even
encouraged. However, God's injunction to Noah to multiply and re-
plenish the earth is hardly the Scripture to apply to a world faced with
a population explosion and at a time when believers can see the approach of the end of the age.

During the Great Tribulation there will be an exaggerated emphasis upon sex, and obviously immorality will prevail. The 144,000 will
have kept themselves aloof from the sins of the Great Tribulation.

Now, considering adultery in the spiritual sense, in the Old Testament idolatry was classified as spiritual fornication. The classic example is in Ezekiel 16 where we find God's severe indictment against
Israel for fornication and adultery—which was idolatry. The 144,000
will also have kept themselves from the worship of the Beast and his
image during the Great Tribulation.

Therefore, the comment, "These are they which were not defiled
with women; for they are virgins," is probably referring to chastity in

both the literal sense and the spiritual sense. And this makes good sense, by the way.

"Firstfruits unto God and to the Lamb" has definite reference to the nation Israel. "For if the casting away of them be the reconciling of the world, what shall the receiving of them be, but life from the dead? For if the firstfruits be holy, the lump is also holy: and if the root be holy, so are the branches" (Rom. 11:15–16). So Israel is described as the firstfruits, especially the 144,000. I believe that they will occupy a unique place in the millennial Kingdom. They evidently will be the vanguard with the Lamb when He returns to set up the Kingdom, as we will see in chapter 19.

"In their mouth was found no lie" means that they did not participate in the big lie of the Beast when he used lying wonders. They didn't fall for his lie. Remember that the Lord Jesus said that if it were possible to deceive the very elect, they would be deceived. But they will not be deceived.

"They are without blemish." Are they without blemish because they have been purified by the Great Tribulation? No. They are without blemish because they are clothed in the righteousness of Christ. And, friend, that's the way I am going to heaven, also. I'm not going to heaven because I think I am good, because I know that I am not good. And don't look down your nose at me, because you are not good either. Both of us are sinners saved by the grace of God.

PROCLAMATION OF THE EVERLASTING GOSPEL

And I saw another angel fly in the midst of heaven, having the everlasting gospel to preach unto them that dwell on the earth, and to every nation, and kindred, and tongue, and people,

Saying with a loud voice, Fear God, and give glory to him; for the hour of his judgment is come: and worship him that made heaven, and earth, and the sea, and the fountains of waters [Rev. 14:6–7].

> *And I saw another angel flying in mid heaven, having an*
> *eternal gospel (good tidings) to proclaim unto (over)*
> *them that dwell (sit) on the earth, and unto (over) every*
> *nation and tribe and tongue and people; and he saith*
> *with a great voice, Fear God and give Him glory, for the*
> *hour of His judgment is come: and worship Him that*
> *made the heaven and the earth and sea and fountains of*
> *water.*

"Another angel" denotes another radical change in protocol of God's communication with the earth. This angel is the first in a parade of six "another" angels mentioned in verses 8–9, 15, and 17–18.

During our age the gospel has been committed to men, and they alone are the messengers of it. Angels would like to give the message of the gospel, but they have not been permitted to do so. At the beginning of the Great Tribulation men are the messengers of God, as the 144,000 reveal. Even the two witnesses with supernatural power could not stand up against Satan, but were removed from the satanic scene of earth. Angels as well as men were the messengers of the Old Testament—". . . the word spoken by angels was stedfast . . ." (Heb. 2:2). The times are so intense in the Great Tribulation period that only angels can get the messages of God through to the world. Angels are indestructible.

"Flying in mid heaven" was a ridiculous statement a few years ago, and some of the critics of the Bible laughed at such a thing. It is no longer a ridiculous statement to a generation that has been treated to television via satellite. Worldwide television is a practical reality so that we don't have to wait for the evening news to learn what is happening in Israel or England or Japan, we can see it just as it is happening. And the angel whom John mentions "flying mid heaven" will serve as a broadcasting station to the entire world.

"An eternal gospel." The question naturally arises, How is this the gospel, since the word *gospel* means "good news"? Is this angel bringing good news? Yes, it is good news to those who are God's children, but it is bad news for the unbelievers.

"Fear God" is the message of this "eternal gospel." That is the message. The writer of the Proverbs said that the fear of the Lord is the beginning of wisdom. In effect, the angel is saying to God's people, "Get wise, get smart, because you need to *fear* God. God saved you by His grace, but He is going to judge this earth." This is God's final call before the return of Christ in judgment.

PRONOUNCEMENT OF JUDGMENT ON BABYLON

In this chapter God is bringing before us those who will appear again in the Book of Revelation, but He is giving us now more or less of a program which He is going to follow.

And there followed another angel, saying, Babylon is fallen, is fallen, that great city, because she made all nations drink of the wine of the wrath of her fornication [Rev. 14:8].

And another angel, a second, followed saying, Fell, fell is Babylon the great, that hath made all the nations to drink of the wine of the wrath of her fornication.

There is a book entitled *The Two Babylons,* by Alexander Hislop, which you ought to read. It is especially pertinent in these days in which you and I live. It reveals that Babylon has been Satan's headquarters from the very beginning. Babylon is the place where idolatry began. Semiramis was the wife of Nimrod; some scholars think that she was his mother and that she married her own son. She was queen of Babel, which later became Babylon, and she devised a nice little story (beginning a whole system of idolatry) in which she came out of an egg in the Euphrates River—she cracked the shell and stepped out fully grown. The worship of Semiramis introduced the female principle in the deity. This reveals that Babylon was the fountainhead of false religions.

"Fell, fell is Babylon." This second angel runs ahead and announces that which is yet to come as though it had already taken place. In the original Greek, "fell" is in the prophetic aorist tense. In other words, God's prophetic word is so sure that He speaks as though the event had already taken place. It is just as sure as if it were history already.

The city of Babylon will evidently be rebuilt during the Great Tribulation period. If you have my book on Isaiah, you will see that I deal with the probability in chapter 13. I believe that ancient Babylon will be rebuilt, though not at the same location, and that judgment upon it, which is predicted in the Book of Isaiah, is yet to come.

The idolatry of Babylon is a divine intoxication which will fascinate the entire world. This is the reason we are seeing so much experimentation in our day with Satan worship, exorcism, and all the cults which are definitely satanic. Notice what the Old Testament prophets have said about it: "Babylon hath been a golden cup in the LORD'S hand, that made all the earth drunken: the nations have drunken of her wine; therefore the nations are mad" (Jer. 51:7). If you could get away far enough and look back at this earth, I am of the opinion that you would be disappointed in mankind and in the nations of the world. Then in the prophecy of Isaiah we read: "And I will punish the world for their evil, and the wicked for their iniquity; and I will cause the arrogancy of the proud to cease, and will lay low the haughtiness of the terrible" (Isa. 13:11). This brings down the wrath of God upon the world (see Jer. 25:15–26). "And Babylon, the glory of kingdoms, the beauty of the Chaldees' excellency, shall be as when God overthrew Sodom and Gomorrah" (Isa. 13:19).

This is a judgment on Babylon that we are going to see: judgment upon religious Babylon in chapter 17 of Revelation and upon commercial Babylon in chapter 18.

PRONOUNCEMENT OF JUDGMENT ON THOSE WHO RECEIVE THE MARK OF THE BEAST

It is probably true that those who live through all or most of the Great Tribulation do so because they had received the mark of the Beast. However, part of the Great Tribulation is not caused by Satan's being released but by Christ's judgment upon this earth. He will move personally and directly in putting down the rebellion against Him here on this earth.

And the third angel followed them, saying with a loud voice, If any man worship the beast and his image, and receive his mark in his forehead, or in his hand,

The same shall drink of the wine of the wrath of God, which is poured out without mixture into the cup of his indignation; and he shall be tormented with fire and brimstone in the presence of the holy angels, and in the presence of the Lamb:

And the smoke of their torment ascendeth up for ever and ever: and they have no rest day or night, who worship the beast and his image, and whosoever receiveth the mark of his name.

Here is the patience of the saints: here are they that keep the commandments of God, and the faith of Jesus [Rev. 14:9–12].

And another angel, a third, followed them, saying with a great voice, If any man worshipeth the beast and his image, and receiveth a mark on his forehead, or upon his hand, he also shall drink of the wine of the wrath of God, which is mingled unmixed in the cup of His anger; and he shall be tormented with fire and brimstone in the presence of the holy angels, and in the presence of the Lamb; and the smoke of their torment goeth up for ever and ever (unto the ages of the ages); and they have no rest day and night, they that worship the wild beast and his image, and whoso receiveth the mark of his name. Here is the patience of the saints, who keep the commandments of God and the faith of Jesus.

He is speaking to a group of people who "keep the commandments of God," the Old Testament law. Scripture tells us that sacrifices will be brought during the Great Tribulation and even into the Millennium.

This section makes it crystal clear that no one can assume a neutral position during this intense period under the Beast. Even today we see Christian businessmen who are capitulating to the ethics of the hour. In chapter 13 we saw that the awful alternative for refusing to receive the mark of the Beast was starvation. On the other hand, the person who receives the mark brings down upon his head the wrath of God.

"He also shall drink of the wine of the wrath of God." If you believe that the church is going through the Great Tribulation, you also believe that the Lord Jesus Christ is going to subject His own to the mingled, unmixed cup of His anger. I simply cannot believe that Christ would do this to the church which He has redeemed.

"The wine of the wrath of God" is a figure adopted from the Old Testament. In Psalm 75:8 we read: "For in the hand of the LORD there is a cup, and the wine is red; it is full of mixture; and he poureth out of the same: but the dregs thereof, all the wicked of the earth shall wring them out, and drink them." The Old Testament prophets picked up that theme. They saw the cup of wrath filling up to the brim. God was patient and let man go on and on in his sin, but when the cup of wrath was filled, then God would press it to the lips of a godless society. Rebellious men kept building this thing up until judgment had to break.

"Tormented with fire and brimstone." Now let me say that if this is not literal fire and brimstone, whatever it is must be worse than fire and brimstone. If it is a symbol, remember that a symbol is used to give a faint representation of the real. It is rather like the essence of something. There is the essence of pepper and the essence of perfume. Essence is the faint odor that is left in the bottle after the substance is gone. A symbol is an essence or just a faint copy of the real thing, and the reality can be much worse than the symbol indicates. But remember, the brimstone of Sodom was quite literal. That is a fact you should mull over in your mind if you want to reject a literal hell.

You will notice in this passage that hell is visible to Christ and the holy angels. It does not say that hell is visible to the twenty-four elders. Are we to assume from that that the church does not know what is taking place on the earth? I am inclined to believe that the church will not see what is taking place on the earth during the Great Tribulation period, but certainly Christ and the holy angels will see it.

All that God's own can do during this period is to be patient and wait for the coming of Christ. Our Lord said: "But he that shall endure unto the end, the same shall be saved" (Matt. 24:13). Why will he endure? He will endure because he has been sealed by the Spirit of God, and he is clothed in the righteousness of Christ. He is able to overcome by the blood of the Lamb. Our Lord said, "In your patience possess ye your souls" (Luke 21:19). All they can do is wait out the storm, and that is what they will do during the Great Tribulation.

PRAISE FOR THOSE WHO DIE IN THE LORD

Here again is a verse that is taken to a funeral in our day, and certainly to use it at a funeral completely robs it of its application. This verse refers only to the Great Tribulation period:

And I heard a voice from heaven saying unto me, Write, Blessed are the dead which die in the Lord from henceforth: Yea, saith the Spirit, that they may rest from their labours; and their works do follow them [Rev. 14:13].

And I heard a voice from heaven saying, Write, Blessed are the dead who die in the Lord from henceforth: yea, said the Spirit, that they may rest from their labors (sorrows), for their works follow with them.

Apparently many of God's tribulation saints, both of the 144,000 and of the untold number of Gentiles that will be saved during that time, are going to lay down their lives for Christ. They will be martyred. During the time of the Great Tribulation, it will be better to die than to live. At that time this verse will give comfort and assurance. They will have rest from their sorrows, and their works will follow them, and the Lord will reward them.

As I have said, this is not a verse for God's saints in comfortable, affluent America, as I see it. For most of us it is unnatural to want to die. I feel as Paul expressed it: "For I am in a strait betwixt two, having a desire to depart, and to be with Christ; which is far better: nevertheless to abide in the flesh is more needful for you. And having this confidence, I know that I shall abide and continue with you all for your furtherance and joy of faith; that your rejoicing may be more abundant in Jesus Christ for me by my coming to you again" (Phil. 1:23–26).

Personally, I would like to stay down here for quite a few more years and teach the Word of God. I am in no hurry to get to heaven. This old story illustrates my viewpoint: A black boy in my southland years ago went to church on a Sunday night. The preacher asked, "How many of you want to go to heaven?" Everybody but this boy put up his hand. The preacher looked at him and asked, "Son, don't you want to go to heaven?" "Sure," the boy answered, "but I thought you were getting up a load for tonight!"

Well, I don't want to be on that load leaving tonight either. I'm going there ultimately, but I would like to live and serve as long as possible. For me it would be unnatural to want to die, but in the Great Tribulation it will be a different story. They will just be waiting in patience and in sorrow. If they are martyred, it will be a wonderful thing. "Blessed are the dead which die in the Lord." He is going to reward them for their faithfulness to Himself.

You can see that this verse is not appropriate for a funeral, especially for a wealthy man who has been living in clover all of his life. In Texas I heard it used at a rich man's funeral, a man who had been brought up in a home of wealth. He had never known what it was to lift his little finger in actual work. He just toyed around with a ranch and lost money on it—he had so much money, he had to get rid of it some way. Yet the preacher applied this verse to him! That is a terrible abuse of the Word of God. Death is going to be precious to the people in the Great Tribulation but not for the saints of our society in which everything is geared to comfort.

"For their works follow with them" reveals that they will be rewarded for their faithfulness, patience, and works in this period. God does not save anyone for his works, but He does reward us for our works. Our works (good or bad) are like tin cans tied to a dog's tail; we cannot get away from them. They will follow us to the *bema* seat of Christ.

PREVIEW OF ARMAGEDDON

And I looked, and behold a white cloud, and upon the cloud one sat like unto the Son of man, having on his head a golden crown, and in his hand a sharp sickle [Rev. 14:14].

"I looked, and behold" emphasizes the fact that John is not only a hearer but a spectator.

"A white cloud, and upon the cloud one sat like unto the Son of man" is evidently the Lord Jesus Christ. The cloud is a mark of identification: "And then shall appear the sign of the Son of man in heaven: and then shall all the tribes of the earth mourn, and they shall see the Son of man coming in the clouds of heaven with power and great glory" (Matt. 24:30). I think that the "clouds" are the *shekinah* cloud, which is "the sign" in heaven.

"On his head a golden crown" further confirms this One as the Lord Jesus Christ. He is the hero of the Book of Revelation, my friend, and you need this book to get a true picture of Him. He is seen as King—not as Prophet or Priest. His office as King is always connected with His return to the earth.

"A sharp sickle" establishes this and speaks of the judgment of the wicked. Dr. Newell calls attention to something that is quite interesting: he notes that the word *sickle* occurs only twelve times in the Scriptures, of which seven are in the verses of this section. Also, the word *sharp* occurs seven times in the Revelation, and four times in this chapter.

And another angel came out of the temple, crying with a loud voice to him that sat on the cloud, Thrust in thy sickle, and reap: for the time is come for thee to reap; for the harvest of the earth is ripe.

And he that sat on the cloud thrust in his sickle on the earth; and the earth was reaped [Rev. 14:15–16].

> *And another angel came out of the temple, crying in a great voice to the One seated on the cloud. Send forth thy sickle, and reap; for the hour is come to reap; for the harvest of the earth was dried. And He that sat on the cloud cast his sickle upon the earth; and the earth was reaped.*

"Send forth thy sickle, and reap" refers to the judgment of men on the earth. "As therefore the tares are gathered and burned in the fire; so shall it be in the end of this world. The Son of man shall send forth his angels, and they shall gather out of his kingdom all things that offend, and them which do iniquity; and shall cast them into a furnace of fire: there shall be wailing and gnashing of teeth" (Matt. 13:40–42). In Matthew the "harvest" has so long been identified with Christian witnessing, and believers have been urged to pray for laborers for the harvest, that it is difficult for the average Christian to fit this scene into the true context of Scripture. Actually, believers are not urged to harvest today; they are urged to sow, to sow the Word of God.

". . . a sower went forth to sow" (Matt. 13:3) is a picture of Christendom today. The Lord Jesus Christ is the Son of Man. He is the sower and the seed is the Word of God and the field is the world. He is flinging out the seed into the world. There is going to be a harvest someday, but that will come at the end of the age. You and I are not in the harvesting business today. Our business is to sow the seed. That is the reason I do not worry about results. I worry a great deal about the source. I want to do my best in giving out the Word of God. Why? Because sowing seed is my business. I am not really concerned about the number of folk who claim to have been converted through my ministry. I just sow the seed. Christ is the One who is going to have the harvest, and the harvest is the judgment at the end of the age. This is the picture given to us here in the Revelation.

Note God's instructions to His Son in the Old Testament: "I will declare the decree: the LORD hath said unto me, Thou art my Son; this day have I begotten thee. Ask of me, and I shall give thee the heathen for thine inheritance, and the uttermost parts of the earth for thy possession. Thou shalt break them with a rod of iron; thou shalt dash them in pieces like a potter's vessel" (Ps. 2:7–9). Did this take place at the Lord's first coming? No. This is no missionary text. When, then, will it take place? It will take place at Christ's second coming to earth. At that time He will come in judgment.

"For the hour is come to reap" is in conformity to the words of Jesus, ". . . the harvest is the end of the world . . ." (Matt. 13:39). The time will come to reap, so let's sow the seed today, and let's not be so everlastingly busy trying to get somebody's hand up and have that one come forward to receive Christ as Savior. Let's make sure that we give out the Word of God, and the Spirit of God will take care of the results.

The time of harvest is set before us in the Old Testament: "Put ye in the sickle, for the harvest is ripe: come, get you down; for the press is full, the vats overflow; for their wickedness is great. Multitudes, multitudes in the valley of decision: for the day of the LORD is near in the valley of decision" (Joel 3:13–14).

And another angel came out of the temple which is in heaven, he also having a sharp sickle.

And another angel came out from the altar, which had power over fire; and cried with a loud cry to him that had the sharp sickle, saying, Thrust in thy sharp sickle, and gather the clusters of the vine of the earth; for her grapes are fully ripe [Rev. 14:17–18].

And another angel came out from the sanctuary which is in heaven, he also having a sharp sickle. And another angel came out from the altar, he that hath (having) power over the fire, and he called with a great voice to him that had the sharp sickle, saying, Send forth thy sharp sickle, and gather the clusters of the vine of the earth; for her grapes are fully ripe.

"The sanctuary which is in heaven" identifies this with the Old Testament, not with the church.

The "sharp sickle" indicates judgment. "Her grapes are fully ripe" conveys the thought of their being dry like raisins. This is a change of metaphor for the War of Armageddon, and this is the picture Isaiah gives: "Who is this that cometh from Edom, with dyed garments from Bozrah? this that is glorious in his apparel, travelling in the greatness of his strength? I that speak in righteousness, mighty to save. Wherefore art thou red in thine apparel, and thy garments like him that treadeth in the winevat? I have trodden the winepress alone; and of the people there was none with me: for I will tread them in mine anger, and trample them in my fury; and their blood shall be sprinkled upon my garments, and I will stain all my raiment. For the day of vengeance is in mine heart, and the year of my redeemed is come. And I looked, and there was none to help; and I wondered that there was none to uphold: therefore mine own arm brought salvation unto me; and my fury, it upheld me. And I will tread down the people in mine anger, and make them drunk in my fury, and I will bring down their strength to the earth" (Isa. 63:1–6).

This vivid picture is not of Christ at His first coming but of Christ when He returns in judgment. In Isaiah's day men would get into the winepress barefooted to tread out the grapes. The red juice would spurt out of the ripe grapes and stain their garments. The picture in this verse is of spectators seeing that there is blood on our Lord's beautiful garments as though He had trodden the winepress. When Christ came the first time, He shed His blood for them, but they have rejected it. Now He is trodding down the wicked, and it is their blood that is shed. He will gather them, as we will see in Revelation 16:16, "into a place called in the Hebrew tongue Armageddon." It is not a single battle but a war—the War of Armageddon (Heb.: Har-Magedon).

Notice in this passage from Isaiah's prophecy that He is seen treading the winepress alone. It is positively terrifying. Little wonder that the men of this earth will cry to the rocks to fall upon them and hide them from the wrath of the Lamb. This will be the sad end of that civilization which at the Tower of Babel demonstrated an active rebellion against God, a rebellion which has been mounting like a mighty crescendo ever since and will break in all of its fury during the Great Tribulation period. As we will see when we come to chapter 19, when Christ comes He will put down that rebellion against God in order to establish His Kingdom here upon the earth. He will (in the language of Psalm 2) "break them with a rod of iron" and "dash them in pieces like a potter's vessel."

You see, the "gentle Jesus" who wouldn't swat a fly, whom we have heard so much about, is just not the Jesus of the Word of God. The Lord Jesus Christ is the *Savior* of the world, but He is also the *Judge* of all the world. If you do not accept His blood shed for you, then if the Great Tribulation period comes during your lifetime, your blood will be shed.

My feeling is that no careful study of the Word of God would lead any person of reasonable intelligence to believe that the church is going through this awful period. Folk who want to push the church into the Great Tribulation seem to think that it will be no more unpleasant than a trip to the dentist to get a tooth pulled. Such a trip is not pleasant; no one enjoys having a tooth pulled, but it can be endured. My friend, if that is in your thinking, you just haven't seen what the Tribulation really will be. Isaiah gives us another picture of it: "Come near, ye nations, to hear; and hearken, ye people: let the earth hear, and all that is therein; the world, and all things that come forth of it. For the indignation of the LORD is upon all nations, and his fury upon all their armies: he hath utterly destroyed them, he hath delivered them to the slaughter. Their slain also shall be cast out, and their stink shall come up out of their carcases, and the mountains shall be melted with their blood. . . . The sword of the LORD is filled with blood, it is made fat with fatness, and with the blood of lambs and goats, with the fat of the kidneys of rams: for the LORD hath a sacrifice in Bozrah, and a great slaughter in the land of Idumea" (Isa. 34:1–3, 6).

What a picture this is! The *precious blood* of the Lamb having been rejected, the blood of those who defied God and followed and worshiped the Beast bathes the earth. It is frightful. As a ripe grape is mashed and the juice flies in every direction, so will little man fall into the vat of God's judgment. This is Armageddon—the mount of slaughter.

And the angel thrust in his sickle into the earth, and gathered the vine of the earth, and cast it into the great winepress of the wrath of God.

And the winepress was trodden without the city, and blood came out of the winepress, even unto the horse bridles, by the space of a thousand and six hundred furlongs [Rev. 14:19–20].

And the angel cast his sickle into the earth, and gathered the vine of the earth, and cast it into the winepress, the great winepress of the wrath of God. And the winepress was trodden without the city, and there came out blood from the winepress, even unto the bridles of the horses, as far as a thousand and six hundred furlongs.

"Without the city" means outside of Jerusalem.

"Unto the bridles of the horses" means about four feet deep.

"A thousand and six hundred furlongs" is about 185 miles, and that is the distance from Dan to Beer-sheba. All of Palestine is the scene of this final war which ends in what is called Armageddon. It is a campaign beginning about the middle of the Great Tribulation and is concluded by the personal return of Christ to the earth. Psalm 45:3–7 is an Old Testament prediction of this: "Gird thy sword upon thy thigh, O most mighty, with thy glory and thy majesty. And in thy majesty ride prosperously because of truth and meekness and righteousness; and thy right hand shall teach thee terrible things. Thine arrows are sharp in the heart of the king's enemies; whereby the people fall under thee. Thy throne, O God, is for ever and ever: the sceptre of thy kingdom is a right sceptre. Thou lovest righteousness, and hatest wickedness: therefore God, thy God, hath anointed thee with the oil of gladness above thy fellows." Psalm 45 is a messianic psalm.

Let me make it clear that I make no apology for these scenes of judgment. God has not asked me to apologize for His Word. He has told me to give it out. We need to face up to the facts:

1. Sin is an awful thing.
2. Sin is in the world.
3. You and I are sinners. The only remedy for sin is the redemption Christ offered when He shed His blood on the cross and paid the penalty for our sins.

4. You and I merit the judgment of God. Our only escape is to accept the work of Christ for us on Calvary's cross. The Bible asks a question that even God cannot answer: "How shall we escape, if we neglect so great salvation? . . ." (Heb. 2:3). Escape what? Escape judgment—the Tribulation is *judgment*. The way out is to accept Christ. Call it an escape mechanism if you want to; but, my friend, when the house is on fire, I'll go out a window or any other way that is an escape. This judgment must inevitably come on Christ-rejectors. Mankind has rejected Him, trodden under foot the Son of God, and counted the blood of the covenant as an unholy thing. If God is just (and He is) there will be *judgment*. The generation of today needs to hear this. Instead of being given this, they are offered endless little methods of living the Christian life. My friend, there is nothing that will straighten out your life like knowing that our God is a holy God, that the Lord Jesus Christ is righteous, and that He is *not* going to tolerate sin in your life.

And this same concept should be taught to our children. I am heartened to see that some psychologists are returning to this position. My friend, the problem with your little Willie is that he is a mean little brat and should be turned across your knee and spanked instead of being treated as a cross between a piece of Dresden china and an orchid. As someone has well said, the board of education should be applied to the seat of learning.

Before we leave this chapter, I would like to draw your attention again to the viewpoint which is abroad concerning the church's going through the Great Tribulation period. I have an article from a magazine that presents this viewpoint. The author of the article is a layman, and yet he has the audacity to write the following:

> There is a shallow Christianity moving across our land. Those who do not have deep roots in Christ shrink from the idea that God would test His people with the Tribulation, or that He would use suffering to help the church make herself ready as a Bride for Christ. Very clearly, though, suffering is the pathway to glory. We are called to it. Why? "Because Christ also suffered, leaving us an example that we should follow in His

steps." As a result of this thinking, I no longer teach Christians they will not have to go through the Tribulation. Maybe they won't, but I can do more for them by preparing them to face testing in His name than by teaching them that the Lord is going to rapture them out of the hour of trial.

In his article this layman also says, "There is a tremendous growth in that person who puts on the whole armor of God, that he may be able to withstand in the evil day." My friend, I want you to know that the Great Tribulation is not called the "evil day." It is called the great day of God's wrath. That is how the Tribulation is described in the Bible. I don't know how anyone could read and study the Book of Revelation and believe that going through the Great Tribulation would *purify* the church or that the bride has to make herself ready! What do you think Christ did when He died on the cross? He made us ready there. We can never become *worthy* to enter into the presence of God. We are going to enter His presence "in Christ," and you can't add anything to that. You can't equate the hour of trial with the great day of the wrath of God that is going to come on this earth. The church will be delivered from that. The Book of Revelation has made that clear. The 144,000 have already been identified for us as Israelites, and even the tribes are identified for us, so there is no way in the world of saying that this group is the church; nor is that great company "which no man could number" the church, the bride of Christ (see Rev. 7:9).

We have seen that God was able to keep the 144,000 during the Great Tribulation. So it is not a question of whether God *can* keep the church in the Great Tribulation period. Of course, He can keep the church if that is His will and plan. But, according to the Word of God, this is *not* His will and plan. The Lord Jesus said, "I am going to keep you *from* that hour that is coming on this earth," from that terrible time of testing that is coming. I would like to put it like this: The church is not going through the *Great* Tribulation period, but we are going through the *little* tribulation. All of us have troubles and trials, and I don't know of a Christian who doesn't have problems and difficulties. It seems like the more spiritually mature the saint of God is, the more he suffers. This is the method God uses to develop his children. We never become wonderful saints of God. We are just His little children, immature and undeveloped. When we come into His presence, we will be accepted because of what *Christ* has done for us, not because we have endured the Great Tribulation.

Another point to consider is that *most* of the church has already missed the Great Tribulation. For over nineteen hundred years believers have been going into the presence of Christ through the doorway of death. I hope you don't believe that God is going to send them back to earth so they can go through the Great Tribulation period! At best there will be only a small percentage of believers who are still alive when the time of tribulation comes upon the earth. The great majority of the church has already missed the Great Tribulation.

I have always had the impression that the folk who believe that the church will go through the Great Tribulation feel that our crowd needs it, and specifically that *I* need it, that I deserve to go through it. Well, I agree that I do deserve it, and I also deserve hell. But I'm not going to hell because Christ bore it for me, and I have trusted in Him. Neither am I going through the Great Tribulation. Why? Because Christ died for me, and He saves me by His grace. Isn't the One who says that He is rich in grace able to deliver me out of the Great Tribulation?

It is true that God allows us to go through the little tribulation of this life. After having cancer and several major operations, I feel as if I have been through the little tribulation period. And it is by this method that God refines us and purifies us. A preacher friend said to me recently, "I can tell a difference in your ministry since you have gone through those illnesses." I trust that he is correct in that. I know God allowed it for a purpose.

When I read the article by the brother who thinks the church should go through the Great Tribulation, I wondered if he had ever really suffered for Christ. A preacher friend of mine who holds this view was discussing it as we were having lunch together one day. As he was eating a T-bone steak, he talked as nonchalantly about the Great Tribulation as if it would not be any worse than the church wading through a river or enduring a very hot summer or experiencing an energy shortage. He apparently did not think of it as being the terrible time which is depicted in the Book of Revelation. Is God misrepresenting the facts to us? Is He just trying to scare us?

Well, my friend, there are places in this book where God uses symbols. Do you know why He uses symbols? He doesn't do it in order to evaporate the facts so that we can dismiss them, but because the reality which the symbol represents is lots worse than the symbol. Many of the things which John tries to describe to us beggar description. Even God cannot communicate some of them to us—not because He is not able, but because we are dull of hearing, as He has told us. We don't always understand. I am afraid that a great many folk just do not realize that the Great Tribulation is a *terrible* thing, and it is *miraculous* that the 144,000 will come through it. He won't lose one of them. Why? Because they will be big, strong, robust fellows? No. They will overcome by the blood of the Lamb. That's how they will do it.

CHAPTER 15

THEME: Preparation for final judgment of the Great Tribulation

In this chapter we have another sign in heaven, seven angels with the seven last plagues. Chapters 15 and 16 belong together because in them we have the pouring out of the seven mixing bowls of wrath. I imagine that you thought the worst was over, but the worst is yet to come. We have already seen the seven seals, the seven trumpets, and the seven personalities. Now the coming seven bowls of wrath are the worst of all. Chapter 15, besides being the shortest chapter in Revelation, is the preface to the final series of judgments which come on the earth during the Great Tribulation. These judgments are the most intense and devastating of any that have preceded them.

The purpose of the Great Tribulation is judgment. It is *not* for the purifying of the church! It is to give Satan his final opportunity. God is going to remove the church before this time of tribulation because of His marvelous, infinite grace. If you are willing to accept His grace, then you can escape the Great Tribulation. Believe me, the bowls of wrath are not the "blessed hope" for which believers are looking. No, we are "Looking for that blessed hope, and the glorious appearing of the great God and our Saviour Jesus Christ" (Titus 2:13). If we will grow in love with Him, we will not consider the judgments of the Great Tribulation terrifying. You don't have to stick your head in the sand like the proverbial ostrich and refuse to read the Book of Revelation. My friend, if you are trusting Christ, you won't be going through it. But you need to know what the unsaved will have to go through, and that might make you a zealous witness for Christ in these difficult days.

Someone said of Dwight L. Moody that in his day he looked into the faces of more people than any man who ever lived and that he reduced the population of hell by two million. We hear a lot of talk about reducing the population explosion of this earth. Well, hell has had a population explosion for many years, and I would like to help reduce that.

Before these angels begin to pour out their bowls of wrath, there may be the question still in the minds of some if any believers were able to stand up against the Antichrist. If that question has not been answered to the satisfaction of the reader, it is answered here. There will be those who will be enabled to stand.

First of all, we will see the preparation for the final judgment of the Great Tribulation.

TRIBULATION SAINTS IN HEAVEN WORSHIP GOD

In the first four verses we see that the Tribulation saints in heaven worship God because He is holy and just. This is another interlude.

And I saw another sign in heaven, great and marvellous, seven angels having the seven last plagues; for in them is filled up the wrath of God [Rev. 15:1].

And I saw another sign in (the) heaven, great and wonderful, seven angels having seven plagues, which are the last, for in them (was) finished the wrath of God.

This will bring us to the end of the Great Tribulation period. I don't know about you, but I will be glad to get to the end of it. And then we will see the coming of Christ to the earth.

"And I saw" assures us that John is still a spectator to these events. He is attending the dress rehearsal of the last act of man's little day upon the earth.

"Another sign" connects this chapter with Revelation 12:1, the first sign which, in the opening of chapter 12, was Israel. These seven angels of wrath are connected with the judgments to follow until Christ comes (see ch. 19). From chapter 12 to the return of Christ is a series of events which are mutually related. This does not mean that there is a chronological order but rather a logical order of retracing the same events with added detail. This method is the personal signature of the Holy Spirit, seen first in Genesis 1—2. In Genesis 1 we are given the account of the Creation, the seven days describing God's handiwork. In chapter 2 the Holy Spirit lifted out the account of the creation of man and went over it again, adding details. It is known as the law of recapitulation, and it runs all the way through the Scriptures. For another example, we have the giving of the Mosaic Law in Exodus and then in Deuteronomy the interpretation of the Law with forty years of experience in the wilderness and a great deal of detail added. Also, when we come to the New Testament, we find not one, not two, but four Gospel records because it takes four to give the many sides of the glorious person of Christ who came to earth over nineteen hundred years ago.

Satan, having been cast into the earth, brings down his wrath upon the remnant of Israel. Also, he makes a final thrust for world domination through the two Beasts. Then God makes a final display of His wrath and concludes earth's sordid tragedy of sin. "The LORD said unto my Lord, Sit thou at my right hand, until I make thine enemies thy footstool" (Ps. 110:1).

"Was finished" in the Greek language is in the prophetic aorist tense, which considers an event in the future as already accomplished.

"The wrath of God" marks the final judgment of the Great Tribulation. God has been slow to anger, but here ends His longsuffering. Judgment in the final stages of the Day of Wrath proceeds from God, not from Satan or the wild Beast. It comes directly from the throne of God. *God will judge.*

And I saw as it were a sea of glass mingled with fire: and them that had gotten the victory over the beast, and over his image, and over his mark, and over the number of his name, stand on the sea of glass, having the harps of God [Rev. 15:2].

And I saw as it were a glassy sea mingled with fire, and them that came off victorious from the wild beast, and from his image, and from the number of his name,

*standing by (on the shore of) the glassy sea, having
harps of God.*

"A glassy sea mingled with fire" represents the frightful persecution
by the Beast during the Great Tribulation period. This is the period of
time, as we have seen, where no man could buy or sell unless he had
the mark of the Beast. It is going to be very difficult to get things to eat
in that day. That is the reason the Lord Jesus, speaking of this period
in His Olivet Discourse, said that whoever would give a cup of cold
water in His name would not lose his reward. You see, anyone in that
day who would give even a cup of cold water to one of the 144,000
would put his life in jeopardy because the Beast would put him to
death for harboring what he would classify as a criminal.

Those will be very difficult days. Again I ask the question: Will
anyone make it through the Great Tribulation? No, they won't unless
they are sealed. Although multitudes will be martyred during this
period—and I think that a great many of the 144,000 will lay down
their lives for Jesus—they will be faithful to Him until death. As we
have seen, *all* of the 144,000 will be with the Lamb on Mount Zion.

"And them that came off victorious"—here are the Tribulation
saints who have come through the fires of persecution on the earth
and yet have not lost their *song.* They have the harps of God, and in
the next couple of verses we will see that they are able to sing, and
they do sing.

How about us today, Christian friend? We are not in the Great Tribulation now and never will be, but even in these days are you having
trouble keeping from your heart just a little root of bitterness? We are
warned against this in Hebrews 12:15 because it is so easy for it to
happen. Maybe this has no application to you, but it does have application to me. When I was in my teens, I came to know the Lord and at
seventeen or eighteen made my decision to study for the ministry. I
expected the Christians to support me in my decision. One wealthy
family in Nashville actually turned against me. I was dating their
daughter at the time, and they didn't want a poor preacher in the family. A teenage boy feels these things most keenly, I guess, but even to

this day I have to fight that little root of bitterness against that class of people who treated me so badly at that time. Now that wasn't tribulation at all. It was a heartbreak, but it was not a Great Tribulation by any means.

What about that little root of bitterness? Are you having a problem with it? I meet people, Christian people, who have let that little root of bitterness spoil their lives to the point that it actually causes them to deteriorate in their Christian life and testimony. I know of a lovely Christian family back East. Something happened that caused them to become very bitter towards another family, and they refused to let it go. That root of bitterness has entered into their lives. I have seen the family sitting in church on Sunday without a smile on one of the faces. Bitterness can ruin your Christian life. We need to pray, in the face of life's circumstances, that there will be no root of bitterness within us.

It is remarkable to see that these Tribulation saints who have lived through the horror of the Great Tribulation have kept their song!

Let me share a poem on prayer with you. It was sent to me by one of our radio listeners.

Unanswered yet? Faith cannot be unanswered.
Her feet were firmly planted on the rock.
Amid the wildest storm she stands undaunted
Nor quails before the loudest thunder shock.

She knows Omnipotence has heard her prayer
And cries, It shall be done sometime, somewhere.
Unanswered yet? Nay, do not say ungranted.
Perhaps your part is not yet wholly done.

The work began when your first prayer was uttered,
And God will finish what He has begun.
If you will keep the incense burning there,
His glory you will see, sometime, somewhere.
                              "Sometime, Somewhere"
                              —Ophelia Guyon Browning

My friend, in this life which you and I are living down here, a little bitterness will come in. What will we do about it? We need to pray. In fact, we need to pray about this more than anything else. If these saints can come through the Great Tribulation and still sing, you and I certainly ought to have a song in our hearts regardless of our circumstances.

The psalmist wrote, "For his anger endureth but a moment; in his favour is life: weeping may endure for a night, but joy cometh in the morning" (Ps. 30:5). I have learned over the years that God will never let anyone cross your pathway, not even an enemy, unless it will teach you a lesson. He permits it for a purpose, for the development of your character. We need to be in prayer that we not fall into the trap of Satan and lose the joy of our salvation.

> **And they sing the song of Moses the servant of God, and the song of the Lamb, saying, Great and marvellous are thy works, Lord God Almighty; just and true are thy ways, thou King of saints.**
>
> **Who shall not fear thee, O Lord, and glorify thy name? for thou only art holy: for all nations shall come and worship before thee; for thy judgments are made manifest [Rev. 15:3–4].**

> And they sing the song of Moses the servant of God, and the song of the Lamb, saying, Great and wonderful are thy works, Lord God, the Almighty; righteous and true are thy ways, thou King of the ages (nations). Who shall not fear, Lord, and glorify thy name? For thou only art holy; for all the nations shall come and worship before thee; for thy righteous acts were made manifest.

If you want to learn "the song of Moses," you will find it in Exodus 15:1–21 and Deuteronomy 32:1–43. Both songs speak of God's deliverance, salvation, and faithfulness. "The song of the Lamb" is the ascription of praise to Christ as the Redeemer. We have seen that in Revelation 5:9–12.

Again let me call your attention to the fact that the Book of Revelation is Christocentric, that is, Christ-centered. Don't let the four horsemen carry you away, or don't be distracted by the blowing of the trumpets or by the seven performers. And don't let your interest center on these bowls of wrath. Let's keep our eyes centered on Christ. He is in charge; He is the Lord. In this book we have the unveiling of Jesus Christ in His holiness, in His power, and in His glory. The Man Christ Jesus is wonderful! He is the One who can put His hand in the hand of God and who can put His other hand in the hand of man and bring them together. He can do this because He is God.

"King of the ages" has two other renderings, *King of saints* and *King of the nations.* Any rendering indicates that Christ will be the object of universal worship and acknowledgment. There will be no place where He will not be worshiped.

"Who shall not fear, Lord, and glorify thy name?" In our day there is very little reverential fear of God, even among believers. We have been caught up in this love attitude, and I don't think we should lose sight of the fact that God is love. But God is also light, which means He is holy. God is moving in on churches and dealing with Christians as I have never seen Him do before. I am one Christian who can testify to that. If you are God's child, you had better not do as you please. If you think God would mind sending you a little trouble, you are wrong. God is to be *feared.* Our God is a *holy* God.

"Nations shall come and worship before thee." The day will come when nations will come and worship before the Lord Jesus Christ. This is not true of nations today. That little prayer breakfast in Washington is a pretty sorry substitute for universal worship of God. One man used that prayer breakfast as an argument that we are living in a Christian nation. What nonsense! We are not living in a Christian nation, but there will come a day when every nation will worship Him. This knowledge should cause us to take heart as we see our own nation moving in the wrong direction. The day will come when God will remove the rebellious men and leave only those who will worship Him.

In Psalm 2:8 we read, "Ask of me, and I shall give thee the heathen [nations] for thine inheritance, and the uttermost parts of the earth for thy possession." The nations are going to be His. And in Isaiah 11:9: "They shall not hurt nor destroy in all my holy mountain: for the earth shall be full of the knowledge of the LORD, as the waters cover the sea." In that day there will be no need for our Thru the Bible study because all men are going to have a knowledge of God. In Jeremiah 23:5 we are told, "Behold, the days come, saith the LORD, that I will raise unto David a righteous Branch, and a King shall reign and prosper, and shall execute judgment and justice in the earth."

It is true that our country has been through awful travail, but we have been so engrossed in our own problems that our hearts have grown weary from all the scandal. Other nations, however, have had this same problem. Today it is nauseating to see the immorality, the godlessness, and the injustice in the world. If I weren't a Christian, I would be one of the most radical persons you have ever met. As a child of God, I can see what is happening in the world, but I know I cannot remedy one thing. But Christ is going to reign someday, and He is going to execute judgment and justice in the earth. Thank God for that! I get so tired of politicians telling me that they represent me in Washington and that they are going to do what I want them to do— when all the time they are doing everything they can for their own interests. With rare exceptions, this is equally true of each politicial party. In the face of gross immorality and gross injustice, what can we do? Well, all of us who are God's children need to pray for our country and rejoice that there is coming One who will execute justice and judgment upon the earth.

In Philippians 2:9–11 we read this: "Wherefore God also hath highly exalted him, and given him a name which is above every name: That at the name of Jesus every knee should bow, of things in heaven, and things in earth, and things under the earth; and that every tongue should confess that Jesus Christ is Lord, to the glory of God the Father." Those who are in hell will not acknowledge Him as their Redeemer, but they are going to acknowledge that He is the boss, He is running the universe, and it belongs to Him. And they are going to acknowledge the glory of God—they will have to do that.

"For thy righteous acts were made manifest." This testimony, coming from witnesses of this period, is inexpressibly impressive and should settle in the minds of believers the fact that God is *right* in all that He does. What God is doing may not look right to you, but if you don't think God is doing the right thing, you are wrong, not God. We need to adjust our attitudes and our thinking. Notice the testimony of the Psalms: "Oh let the wickedness of the wicked come to an end; but establish the just: for the righteous God trieth the hearts and reins" (Ps. 7:9). "For the righteous LORD loveth righteousness; his countenance doth behold the upright" (Ps. 11:7). "O give thanks unto the LORD, for he is good: for his mercy endureth for ever. . . . He poureth contempt upon princes, and causeth them to wander in the wilderness, where there is no way. . . . The righteous shall see it, and rejoice: and all iniquity shall stop her mouth" (Ps. 107:1, 40, 42). This will happen when God takes charge.

TABERNACLE OPENED IN HEAVEN FOR ANGELS WITH SEVEN BOWLS

At this point the temple of the tabernacle is opened in heaven in order that seven angels, having seven golden bowls, might proceed forth.

And after that I looked, and, behold, the temple of the tabernacle of the testimony in heaven was opened:

And the seven angels came out of the temple, having the seven plagues, clothed in pure and white linen, and having their breasts girded with golden girdles [Rev. 15:5–6].

And after these things I saw, and the sanctuary (temple) of the tabernacle [Gr.: skenes] of the testimony (witness) in (the) heaven was opened; and there came out from the temple (the) seven angels, having the seven plagues, clothed in linen (precious stone) pure and white, and girt about the breast with golden girdles.

The "temple" is referred to fifteen times in the Book of Revelation. Its prominence cannot be ignored. In the first part of Revelation, through chapter 3, the church is the subject and there is no mention of a temple. Beginning with chapter 4 the scene shifts to heaven, and we see the temple in heaven; also there is a temple on earth patterned after the one in heaven. There is no temple in New Jerusalem where the church is going. Why? Because the church is not identified with a temple. This fact makes it abundantly clear that, beginning with chapter 4, God is dealing with people who have had a temple, and only to Israel had God given a temple, patterned after the one in heaven. In this instance, the reference is specifically to the tabernacle (skenes) and the Holy of Holies in which the ark of the testimony was kept. In the ark were the tables of stone. Both the tabernacle and the tables of stone were duplicates of originals in heaven. "And look that thou make them after their pattern, which was shewed thee in the mount" (Exod. 25:40). "It was therefore necessary that the patterns of things in the heavens should be purified with these; but the heavenly things themselves with better sacrifices than these" (Heb. 9:23).

The originals are referred to in Revelation 11:19: "And the temple of God was opened in heaven, and there was seen in his temple the ark of his testament: and there were lightnings, and voices, and thunderings, and an earthquake, and great hail." The action of God here is based on the violation of His covenant with Israel—the broken Law. God is righteous in what He is about to do. He will judge, then He will carry out His covenant with Israel.

The prominence of angels in this book is again called to our attention by the appearance of angels at this point. Previously, seven angels blew on seven trumpets. Here is the new series of seven angels who have the seven plagues of the seven bowls of wrath. The departure of the angels from the temple demonstrates that they depart from the throne of mercy, and now God acts in justice instead of in mercy.

"Clothed in linen." The angels are clothed in linen—another meaning is clothed with precious stones. It is an enigmatic expression due to a variant reading in the text. Were they clothed in linen or a stone? The intention, it seems, is to describe their garments as studded and set with precious stones. Though their garments identify them in a priestly activity, they forsake that work of mercy for plagues of judgment.

The "golden girdles" reveal the angels in the livery of Christ, who no longer is exercising a priestly function but is seen here judging the world.

> **And one of the four beasts gave unto the seven angels seven golden vials full of the wrath of God, who liveth for ever and ever.**
>
> **And the temple was filled with smoke from the glory of God, and from his power; and no man was able to enter into the temple, till the seven plagues of the seven angels were fulfilled [Rev. 15:7–8].**

> *And one of the four living creatures gave to the seven angels seven golden bowls, full of the wrath of God, who liveth for ever and ever. And the sanctuary (temple) was filled with smoke from the glory of God, and from his power; and no one was able to enter into the sanctuary (temple), till the seven plagues of the seven angels should be finished.*

"Seven angels seven golden vials." Again let me call your attention to the repetition of the number seven. I sometimes hear it said that seven is the number of perfection, which is not exactly accurate. It is the number of completeness, and sometimes completeness is perfection. For example, in six days God created heaven and earth and rested on the seventh day—not only because it was complete, but because it was perfect. But here in the Revelation the series of sevens denotes a completion. My feeling is that we have a complete history of the church in the seven churches, and that we have a complete Great Tribulation period in each one of the series of sevens; in other words, each covers it all. First, in the seven seals we see a broad outline, then, as we read along in the prophecy, we see that God zeroes in and focuses on the last three and a half years.

"Bowls (vials), full of the wrath of God." Notice, they are not filled with the *love* of God but with God's *wrath*.

"The sanctuary (temple) was filled with smoke from the glory of God." The very fact that this section continues to deal with the temple ought to indicate to anyone who is knowledgeable that the church is not involved. Neither the temple nor the tabernacle had anything to do with the church. They present marvelous pictures of Christ which have spiritual applications for us today, but that does not mean that the church should build a temple or a tabernacle. Rather, this section refers to Israel, a people who had a tabernacle and a temple. A great many are reluctant to admit this fact because they dismiss Israel from the plan and purpose of God at the beginning of the New Testament. As you can see, the New Testament by no means dismisses Israel!

The "seven golden bowls" represent the final part of the Great Tribulation period. I think that "bowls" better describes the container than "vials"—a vial makes me think of a little test tube that is used in a laboratory. Bowls were used in the service of the temple. For example, a bowl of blood was taken by the high priest one day each year into the Holy of Holies. And that bowl of blood spoke of redemption for sin.

These seven angels with priestly garments, having departed from the temple proper, are no longer engaged in a service of mercy but are beginning a strange ministry of pouring out bowls of wrath on a Christ-rejecting world. A world that has rejected the blood of Christ must bear the judgment for sin. This judgment is not the result of man's or Satan's enmity. It is the direct action of the Lord Jesus Christ. We have seen the gentle Jesus, and now we see the wrath of the Lamb. You never think of a little lamb as being angry. A lion can roar, but not a little lamb. The wrath of the Lamb is going to startle the world some-day.

The prophets of the Old Testament used the figure of the cup of iniquity and wrath filling up and spoke of God's patience in waiting for it to fill. Then, when it is full, God moves in judgment.

These seven angels with seven golden bowls make it clear that the judgments of the bowls proceed from God and are not the result of man's mistakes or of Satan's enmity. These judgments are the direct action of God.

CHAPTER 16

THEME: Pouring out the seven bowls

The seven angels pouring out the seven bowls of God's wrath upon the earth is the theme of this chapter. Also, it includes the interlude between the sixth and seventh bowls. Chapter 15 was the prelude to this chapter and is organically connected with it.

It is worth repeating that the bowls of wrath contain the direct judgment of God upon the world; they do not proceed from either man's misdoings or Satan's machinations. They are poured out during the reign of the Beast. They cover a very brief period of time, comparatively speaking.

There is a definite similarity between the judgments in this chapter and God's judgments upon Egypt through Moses.

PREPARATION FOR FINAL JUDGMENT OF THE GREAT TRIBULATION

The first verse of this chapter speaks of the message the great voice gives the seven angels.

> **And I heard a great voice out of the temple saying to the seven angels, Go your ways, and pour out the vials of the wrath of God upon the earth [Rev. 16:1].**

As usual, I'll give the literal translation of the Greek text throughout this chapter.

> *And I heard a great voice out of the sanctuary (temple) saying to the seven angels, Go and pour out the seven bowls of the wrath of God into the earth.*

Let me remind you that the Lord Jesus Christ is still in full charge. Remember that way back in chapter 5 the Lord Jesus was the only One found worthy to open the seven-sealed book, and His opening of the seals ushered in this entire series of sevens. He is in command to the end of this book. He is the One who is marching to victory. The power and the glory and the majesty belong to Him. This is His judgment upon a Christ-rejecting world. The Father has committed all judgment unto Him. Christ is the One who gives the command that sends out these seven angels with the final judgments. There is no longer a delay, no longer an interval or intermission. The hour has come. The order is given, and the seven angels execute the command.

It is difficult for man, even Christians, to believe that God is going to pour out His wrath on a rebellious and God-hating world and destroy this civilization. But, my friend, everything you see today is under the judgment of God.

When Mrs. McGee and I first came to Southern California, we almost thought that we had entered the Millennium. Those were the good old days before the great population came, before we had smog and heavy traffic. I still love California, but it is not like it was then. Every Monday we would take the day off and go to see some of the sights. We would drive to the beach, to the mountains, or to the desert. One evening as we were driving down Wilshire Boulevard, a very attractive street, all around us we could see liquor signs and the world of glamour designed to satiate the demands of the flesh. I was reminded of what the Lord Jesus said to the apostles when they came to Him to show Him the buildings of the temple, how beautiful they were. He said to them, "See ye not all these things? verily I say unto you, There shall not be left here one stone upon another, that shall not be thrown down" (Matt. 24:2). They were amazed that He would make a statement like that. And I said to my wife, "All of this beauty and glamour that we are seeing is going to pass away. It is under the judgment of God. It all is going up in smoke someday." Believe me, we need to make our investments in heaven where neither moth nor rust doth corrupt, and where thieves do not break through nor steal. Perhaps you are saying, "But I have gilt-edged investments and bonds in a safety deposit box." Yes, but you are still going to lose them because you are going to leave them. You are going to release your hand in death. You are going to turn them loose and move out.

This world in which we are living is under the judgment of God. It is hard for even believers to accept that fact. After almost a century of insipid preaching from America's pulpits, the average man believes that God is all sweetness and light and would not discipline or punish anyone. Well, this Book of Revelation tells a different story!

POURING OUT OF THE FIRST BOWL

And the first went, and poured out his vial upon the earth; and there fell a noisome and grievous sore upon the men which had the mark of the beast, and upon them which worshipped his image [Rev. 16:2].

And the first went and poured out his bowl into the earth; and it became (there broke out) a noisome and grievous sore upon the men that had the mark of the wild beast, and that worshiped his image.

Vincent writes in his *Word Studies in the New Testament*, "Each angel, as his turn comes, withdraws from the heavenly scene." In other words, the angel leaves the place of the mercy seat in heaven and executes judgment. He leaves heaven and pours a judgment bowl of wrath upon the earth.

The first bowl of judgment is quite interesting. It looks as though God is engaged in germ warfare upon the followers of Antichrist. Scripture states that the life of the flesh is in the blood, and also *death* is in the blood. These putrifying sores are worse than leprosy or cancer. As man discovers a remedy for one disease, another that is more frightful appears. These are judgments of God by which He reveals physically what man is morally—utterly corrupt.

The first bowl of wrath compares to the sixth plague in Egypt and is the same type of sore or "boil" (see Exod. 9:8–12). It is interesting to note that Moses predicted coming judgment upon Israel similar to this. It has not as yet been fulfilled. This prediction is found in the Book of Deuteronomy: "But it shall come to pass, if thou wilt not hearken unto the voice of the LORD thy God, to observe to do all his commandments and his statutes which I command thee this day; that all these curses shall come upon thee, and overtake thee" (Deut. 28:15). Now here is a list of them: "The LORD will smite thee with the botch of Egypt, and with the emerods, and with the scab, and with the itch, whereof thou canst not be healed" (Deut. 28:27). These diseases are incurable, according to Deuteronomy 28:35: "The LORD shall smite thee in the knees, and in the legs, with a sore botch that cannot be healed, from the sole of thy foot unto the top of thy head." These are predictions of Moses.

Now here in the Book of Revelation, the "noisome and grievous sore" is for those who received the mark of the Beast. As we have already seen, those who did not receive the mark have been in a bad way also. They have not been able to buy or sell. If a man has a starving family, I'm not going to blame him for breaking into a market to get food for them. It has been a desperate time for those who have refused the mark. But now, at the end of the Great Tribulation, those who have the mark and have enjoyed all the privileges it brought are going to be judged by God.

May I add a personal comment here: I have always felt that my first bout with cancer was a judgment from God. I still feel the same way today. The fact that God healed me is a sign that He forgave me, and He has given me my greatest ministry since then. I am rejoicing in that. But during the Great Tribulation, God's judgment of this terrible sore—which is probably worse than cancer—does not cause men to turn to God.

POURING OUT OF THE SECOND BOWL

And the second angel poured out his vial upon the sea; and it became as the blood of a dead man; and every living soul died in the sea [Rev. 16:3].

This plague is more severe than that of the second trumpet, where only one-third of the sea became blood. Here it is the *total* sea, and the blood is that of a dead man!

Blood is the token of life. "For the life of the flesh is in the blood . . ." (Lev. 17:11). The sea is a great reservoir of life. It is teeming with life, and the salty water is a cathartic for the filth of the earth. However, in this plague, blood is the token of death; the sea becomes a grave of death instead of a womb of life. The cool sea breezes become a stench from the carcasses floating on the surface of the bloody water and lining the shore. Commerce is paralyzed. Human beings die like flies. The first plague in Egypt was the turning of the waters of the Nile River into blood (see Exod. 7:20–25). There is a striking similarity here.

I wonder if we realize how much we are dependent upon God today? The light company, the gas company, the water company send us bills, but where did they get the light, the gas, and the water? It is obvious that these companies have something to do with getting these things to us, but God was the One who created the light and the gas and the water. Has God ever sent you a bill for the sunshine, for the water you drink, and the air you breathe? Have you paid Him? He has not sent His bill, and you would not be able to pay it if He did. God, who has been so gracious to a Christ-rejecting world, will at last judge all the earth. The angels pour out the bowls in the day of God's wrath.

POURING OUT OF THE THIRD BOWL

And the third angel poured out his vial upon the rivers and fountains of waters; and they became blood.

And I heard the angel of the waters say, Thou art righteous, O Lord, which art, and wast, and shalt be, because thou hast judged thus.

For they have shed the blood of saints and prophets, and thou hast given them blood to drink; for they are worthy.

And I heard another out of the altar say, Even so, Lord God Almighty, true and righteous are thy judgments [Rev. 16:4–7].

And the third angel poured out his bowl into the rivers and the fountains of the waters and it became (there

came) blood. And I heard the angel of the waters saying,
Righteous art thou, who art and who wast, The Holy
One, because thou didst judge these things. For they
shed the blood of saints and prophets, and blood didst
thou give them to drink; they are worthy. And I heard the
altar saying, Yea, the Lord God, the Almighty, true and
righteous are thy judgments.

This plague, similar to that of the third trumpet, again is more severe. There, only one-third of the fresh water was affected, and here
the *total* water supply of the earth will be cut off. This means destruction of human life on an unparelleled plane.

"The angel of the waters" is the superintendent of God's water department here on earth. This reveals another ministry of angels as it
affects creation. They are in charge of the different physical depart-
ments of the universe. We have seen four angels who control the
winds. This angel, who knows the whole story, now declares that God
is right and holy in this act of judgment.

My friend, whatever God does is righteous and holy. If you don't
agree with Him, it is too bad. You are wrong, not God. Imagine a little
man standing up and saying, concerning the Creator, "I don't think
He is doing right." I have a question for the person who would make a
statement like that: "What are you going to do about it? In fact, what
can you do about it?" If you are not in agreement with God, you had
better get in agreement with Him. God is righteous in everything He
does.

"They shed the blood of saints and prophets, and blood didst thou
give them to drink." This is poetic justice with a vengeance. Those
who take the sword will perish by the sword, and the shedding of
blood leads to the shedding of blood. These who are being judged had
made martyrs of God's people, and now God is forcing them to drink
blood for the righteous blood they spilled.

"The altar saying" evidently refers back to the saints under the altar who had been praying for justice to be done: "And when he had
opened the fifth seal, I saw under the altar the souls of them that were
slain for the word of God, and for the testimony which they held: And

they cried with a loud voice, saying, How long, O Lord, holy and true, dost thou not judge and avenge our blood on them that dwell on the earth? And white robes were given unto every one of them; and it was said unto them, that they should rest yet for a little season, until their fellow-servants also and their brethren, that should be killed as they were, should be fulfilled" (Rev. 6:9–11). Here their prayer is answered. God was a long time getting to it, but now the time is come for answering their prayer.

POURING OUT OF THE FOURTH BOWL

And the fourth angel poured out his vial upon the sun; and power was given unto him to scorch men with fire.

And men were scorched with great heat, and blasphemed the name of God, which hath power over these plagues: and they repented not to give him glory [Rev. 16:8–9].

Our Lord predicted signs in the sun during the Great Tribulation: "And there shall be signs in the sun, and in the moon, and in the stars; and upon the earth distress of nations, with perplexity; the sea and the waves roaring" (Luke 21:25).

The Old Testament had a great deal to say about judgment during the Great Tribulation period due to the excessive heat of the sun: "They shall be burnt with hunger, and devoured with burning heat, and with bitter destruction: I will also send the teeth of beasts upon them, with the poison of serpents of the dust" (Deut. 32:24).

Also the prophet Isaiah speaks of this: "Therefore hath the curse devoured the earth, and they that dwell therein are desolate: therefore the inhabitants of the earth are burned, and few men left" (Isa. 24:6). Also—"Therefore he hath poured upon him the fury of his anger, and the strength of battle: and it hath set him on fire round about, yet he knew not; and it burned him, yet he laid it not to heart" (Isa. 42:25).

Back in the prophecy of Malachi we are told: "For, behold, the day cometh, that shall burn as an oven; and all the proud, yea, and all that do wickedly, shall be stubble: and the day that cometh shall burn them up, saith the LORD of hosts, that it shall leave them neither root nor branch" (Mal. 4:1).

To accomplish this, all that the Lord would have to do is to remove one or two blankets of atmosphere. Or He would need only to pull the earth a little closer to the sun—not much—and we would not be able to survive. It is this frightful period that Isaiah had in view when he wrote that the earth would be decimated. And our Lord said, ". . . Except those days should be shortened, there should no flesh be saved . . ." (Matt. 24:22).

Nevertheless, His own are preserved; "The sun shall not smite thee by day, nor the moon by night" (Ps. 121:6). Though this promise is quite meaningless to us today, it will be a great comfort to the believer during the Great Tribulation.

"And men were scorched with great heat, and blasphemed the name of God." In spite of all of this, instead of turning to God for mercy, they blaspheme His name. This reveals that the human heart is incurably wicked. No amount of punishment will purify it and change it. By the same token, the Great Tribulation is not for the purification of the church. Nowhere is it stated that the saints are being purified by the Great Tribulation. Rather, it is a *judgment* upon the earth.

POURING OUT OF THE FIFTH BOWL

And the fifth angel poured out his vial upon the seat of the beast; and his kingdom was full of darkness; and they gnawed their tongues for pain,

And blasphemed the God of heaven because of their pains and their sores, and repented not of their deeds [Rev. 16:10–11].

And the fifth poured out his bowl upon the throne of the wild beast; and his kingdom was darkened, and they chewed their tongues from their pain, and they blasphemed the God of heaven because of their pains and their sores; and they repented not of their works.

"The throne of the wild beast" makes it clear that the first Beast of chapter 13 is a man. He also represents a kingdom, as you cannot have a king without a kingdom.

"His kingdom was darkened" indicates a strange darkness which might be called black light. We are familiar with that in our day. It will be a frightening thing. As the sun's wattage is increased, it grows darker instead of lighter. The heat will be greater, but the light will be less. Note the similarity to the darkness of Egypt during the ninth plague (Exod. 10:21–22).

The Old Testament prophets had a great deal to say about this coming darkness: "For behold, the darkness shall cover the earth, and gross darkness the people: but the LORD shall arise upon thee, and his glory shall be seen upon thee" (Isa. 60:2). "Blow ye the trumpet in Zion, and sound an alarm in my holy mountain: let all the inhabitants of the land tremble: for the day of the LORD cometh, for it is nigh at hand; a day of darkness and of gloominess, a day of clouds and of thick darkness, as the morning spread upon the mountains: a great people and a strong; there hath not been ever the like, neither shall be any more after it, even to the years of many generations. . . . The sun shall be turned into darkness, and the moon into blood, before the great and the terrible day of the LORD come" (Joel 2:1–2, 31).

In addition to these two prophets, Nahum mentions it. Amos mentions it, and Zephaniah mentions it. Now the apostle John is merely saying, "This Great Tribulation period is where these prophecies fit into the program of God." And our Lord Himself confirmed it when He said, "But in those days, after that tribulation, the sun shall be darkened, and the moon shall not give her light" (Mark 13:24).

"They chewed their tongues from their pain." Just think of the intensity of the suffering that is caused by these bowl judgments! But they don't turn men from their wickedness.

There are two self-evident facts at this point: (1) God is righteous in pouring out the bowls of wrath. Let's remember that. Jesus is the judge. He is in charge of handing out the punishment. (2) Yet mankind is not led to repentance through this suffering. The apostle Paul predicted this: "Or despisest thou the riches of his goodness and forbearance and longsuffering; not knowing that the goodness of God leadeth thee to repentance? But after thy hardness and impenitent heart treasurest up unto thyself wrath against the day of wrath and revelation of the righteous judgment of God" (Rom. 2:4–5). And here it is—the righteous judgment of God. And man continues to harden his heart and refuses to repent.

POURING OUT OF THE SIXTH BOWL

And the sixth angel poured out his vial upon the great river Euphrates; and the water thereof was dried up, that the way of the kings of the east might be prepared [Rev. 16:12].

And the sixth poured out his bowl upon the great river, the river Euphrates; and the water was dried up, that the way might be made ready for the kings that come from the sunrising.

The Euphrates is called "the great river" in the Bible just as the Mediterranean Sea is called "the great sea." The prominence of the Euphrates River in the Word of God should not be overlooked. First mentioned in Genesis 2, it is designated over twenty-five times in the Bible. In the verse before us it is seen in connection with the sixth plague. As it was prominent in the first state of man on the earth, so it is featured in his last state—that of the Great Tribulation. It was the cradle of man's civilization and obviously will be the grave of man's civilization. It was a border between East and West, eighteen hundred miles long, over half of it navigable. It was wide and deep, which made it difficult for an army to pass over it.

Abraham was called a Hebrew, and some interpret that as meaning he came from the other side of the Euphrates. The Euphrates was the eastern border of the land God promised to Abraham. "In the same day the Lord made a covenant with Abram, saying, Unto thy seed have I given this land, from the river of Egypt unto the great river, the river Euphrates" (Gen. 15:18). It also became the eastern border of the Roman Empire.

The Euphrates River will be miraculously dried up, thus erasing the border between East and West, so that the kings of the sunrising might come to the Battle of Armageddon. In the past Tamerlane came out of the East and swept across those plains with a tremendous horde, and Genghis Khan did the same thing. Those were just little previews of what is going to happen in the last days. After the Euphrates River is gone, the great hordes in the East that have never moved West will come in a great crusade to Palestine. The bulk of the world population is in the East, and having only a smattering of the gospel, they will choose Antichrist. The picture is frightful. Can anyone doubt, with the hundreds of millions pouring into Palestine, that the blood will be as deep as the horses' bridles?

INTERLUDE: KINGS OF INHABITED EARTH PROCEED TO HAR-MAGEDON

Now between the sixth and seventh bowls of wrath is this interlude. (As I have pointed out, there is interlude, an hiatus, between the sixth and seventh features of each series of seven—with the exception of the seven performers.) It is a break for the filling in of details.

And I saw three unclean spirits like frogs come out of the mouth of the dragon, and out of the mouth of the beast, and out of the mouth of the false prophet.

For they are the spirits of devils, working miracles, which go forth unto the kings of the earth and of the whole world, to gather them to the battle of that great day of God Almighty [Rev. 16:13–14].

And I saw (coming) out of the mouth of the dragon, and out of the mouth of the wild beast, and out of the mouth of the false prophet, as it were frogs. For they are spirits of demons, working signs; which go forth upon the kings of the whole inhabited earth, to gather them together to the war of the great day of the God, the Almighty.

This is Armageddon (more correctly spelled Har-Magedon). It is not to be a single battle but a war, the War of Armageddon.

It will be triggered, I believe, by the coming down of Russia from the north sometime around the middle of the Tribulation period. The campaign extends the length of Palestine to the Valley of Jehoshaphat and the mountains of Edom. It will continue for approximately three and one-half years. It will be concluded by the coming of the Lord Jesus Christ from heaven to establish His Kingdom. The Sun of Righteousness will arise with healing in His wings.

Here we are introduced to the trinity of hell—Satan, Antichrist, and the False Prophet. They act in unison in forcing the nations of the world to march against Israel in an attempt to destroy God's purposes on earth. God gave certain promises to Abraham and to those who would come after him. He made certain covenants with the Hebrew people, and those covenants are going to stand, just like John 3:16 stands for believers today.

I want to say carefully and kindly that there is a system of theology abroad today that passes as conservative, but it takes the position that God is through with the nation Israel, that all of God's covenants with Israel are negated, that God does not intend to make good any of His promises to Israel—yet there are literally hundreds of them in the Old Testament. This theological system simply spiritualizes these promises, and the proponents do so with no scriptural grounds whatsoever. Origen, one of the early church fathers who came from North Africa, started this method of spiritualizing instead of literalizing the Scriptures. We need to remember that the Bible is a literal book. It is the purpose of Satan to destroy God's covenants with Israel, and that is the reason Satan moves in and brings the whole world against this little nation. This will happen during the Great Tribulation.

As the study of prophecy develops, it is my conviction that this spiritualization of prophecy, although presently accepted by a great many expositors, will become a heresy in the church. I may not be around to see it, but just remember that McGee said it would happen.

Now let's look at the tremendous scene before us.

"As it were frogs." The question is: Will they be literal frogs? Well, they were literal in Egypt, and they could be literal in this case, but I am willing to accept them as a symbol. Perhaps you are saying, "Wait a minute, McGee, I thought you didn't accept a symbol unless it was clearly a symbol." Yes, that is right, and notice that John says, "as it were frogs"; he doesn't say they were frogs. It seems to me that John is always very careful to give us an accurate picture of what he sees.

J. A. Seiss, in his book, *The Apocalypse, Lectures on the Book of Revelation,* comments on the frogs in a vivid manner:

> They are spirits; they are "unclean spirits;" they are "demon spirits;" they are sent forth into activity by the Dragon Trinity; they are the elect agents to awaken the world to the attempt to abolish God from the earth; and they are frog-like in that they come forth out of the pestiferous quagmires of the universe, do their work amid the world's evening shadows, and creep, and croak, and fill the ears of the nations with their noisy demonstrations, till they set all the kings and armies of the whole earth in enthusiastic commotion for the final crushing out of the Lamb and all His powers. As in chapter 9, the seven Spirits of God and of Christ went forth into all the earth to make up and gather together into one holy fellowship the great congregation of the sanctified: so these spirits of hell go forth upon the kings and potentates of the world, to make up and gather together the grand army of the Devil's worshippers.

In our own day we have seen that the news media can become a propaganda agent to carry out the purposes of men who are in the background. The news media can brainwash the public. This is exactly what the trinity of evil will do. They will brainwash the nations of the world into marching against Israel.

The Lord Jesus is the only One who can stop this. Israel's help does not come from the North or the South or the East or the West—that's where their trouble is coming from. Their help comes from the Lord, the Maker of heaven and earth.

Behold, I come as a thief. Blessed is he that watcheth, and keepeth his garments, lest he walk naked, and they see his shame [Rev. 16:15].

"Behold, I come as a thief." Christ will never come as a thief to the church: "But ye, brethren, are not in darkness, that that day should overtake *you* as a thief" (1 Thess. 5:4, italics mine). A thief is someone you shut out; you don't welcome him. You don't put a note on the door when you leave your house which says, "Mr. Thief, I left the back door open for you. The silver is on the third shelf; help yourself." You never welcome a thief. You lock him out. Christ does not come as a thief to His church which is looking for Him. "Looking for that blessed hope, and the glorious appearing of the great God and our Saviour Jesus Christ" (Titus 2:13).

The Lord Jesus Christ *does* come as a thief to the world at the end of the Great Tribulation, as the verse before us indicates. As we saw at the beginning of the Revelation, the whole earth will mourn because of Him. They don't want Him to come. They would like to shut Him out from ever returning to the earth.

"Blessed is he that . . . keepeth his garments." What garments are these? Edersheim sheds light on this phrase by explaining that the captain of the temple made his rounds during the night to see if the guards were awake and alert. If one was found asleep, he was either beaten or his garments set on fire. I suppose it could be paraphrased, "Don't lost your shirt. Be sure that you are clothed with the righteousness of Christ."

And he gathered them together into a place called in the Hebrew tongue Armageddon [Rev. 16:16].

This is the only occurrence of the word *Armageddon* in Scripture, although there are many references to it. It means "Mount of Megiddo." It is a compound word made up of the Hebrew words *Har,* meaning "mountain," and *Megiddo,* which is a mount in the plain of Esdraelon. I have been there several times. It is one of the most fertile valleys I have ever seen. I guess it is the most fertile valley in the world today. It is a place where many battles have been fought in the past.

Vincent cites *Clarke's Travels* regarding Megiddo in the plain of Esdraelon:

> ... Which has been a chosen place for encampment in every contest carried on in Palestine from the days of Nabuchodonozor king of Assyria, unto the disastrous march of Napolean Bonaparte from Egypt into Syria. Jews, Gentiles, Saracens, Christian crusaders, and anti-Christian Frenchmen; Egyptians, Persians, Druses, Turks, and Arabs, warriors of every nation that is under heaven, have pitched their tents on the plain of Esdraelon, and have beheld the banners of their nation wet with the dews of Tabor and Hermon.

"He gathered them together." The "he" is possibly God Himself. Although Satan, Antichrist, and the False Prophet act in unison to force the nations of the world to march against Israel, they nevertheless fulfill the Word of God.

POURING OUT OF THE SEVENTH BOWL

And the seventh angel poured out his vial into the air; and there came a great voice out of the temple of heaven, from the throne, saying, It is done.

And there were voices, and thunders, and lightnings; and there was a great earthquake, such as was not since men were upon the earth, so mighty an earthquake, and so great [Rev. 16:17–18].

And the seventh poured out his bowl upon the air; and a great voice came out of the temple, from the throne, saying, It is done. And there were lightnings, and voices and thunders; and there was a great earthquake, such as was not since there were men upon the earth, so great an earthquake, so mighty.

"The seventh poured out his bowl upon the air." This is the last series of seven judgments before the coming of Christ, and this is the seventh and last of the last seven. In other words, we are right at the end of the Great Tribulation here. At this point the only One who could deliver these people and set up a righteous kingdom on earth and bring peace to the world is the Lord Jesus Christ. Let us keep our eyes on Christ through this. He is the judge now.

"Upon the air" means in space, with no specific geographical location. The Lord Jesus Christ controls space. He is getting ready to come through space.

"The temple" has been mentioned again and again and again. It has been mentioned with the bowls of wrath, the trumpets, and the seals; in fact, it has been mentioned with each series of judgments. However, the temple has been mentioned with the bowls of wrath six times—more than with all the other judgments combined—and this is the last reference to it. There is no temple in the New Jerusalem, so this obviously has no reference to the church. Whether we like it or not, Israel will go through the Great Tribulation period. We know that the remnant, all 144,000 of them, will make it through; that is, they will be faithful until death. And I do not know how many more there will be. We do know that a great company of Gentiles were sealed and that they are going to make it through the Great Tribulation also.

Again let me repeat that the church is not a part of this scene. The church is not going through the Time of Jacob's Trouble. God has two ways of saving people in the Great Tribulation period: first, saving them out of it by taking them out of the world, as He took Enoch before the judgment of the Flood; second, by saving them in it, as He preserved the life of Noah during the Flood. God will definitely save people during the days of the Great Tribulation, but the church will not be a part of that, for it will have been taken from the earth before the Tribulation begins.

"A great voice came out of the temple, from the throne." That voice is not identified for us, but I personally believe that it is the voice of none other than the Son of God. His message is recorded: "It is done." This is the second time we have heard Him say this. When He was hanging upon the cross, He said, "It is finished"—in Greek it is one word: *Tetelestai*, "It is done." At that point in history redemption was wrought and salvation was finished for man. There is nothing man can contribute to his salvation; he must simply receive it by faith. You can have a finished redemption; but if you won't accept it, there will be a judgment. For those who have refused God's salvation, there is nothing they can do to escape the judgment of God. It is done. No wonder the writer to the Hebrews wrote: "How shall we escape, if we neglect so great salvation; which at the first began to be spoken by the Lord, and was confirmed unto us by them that heard him . . . ?" (Heb. 2:3). Christ is the judge, and the judgment of the Great Tribulation is now concluded. "It is done" is His announcement, and there is nothing ahead but judgment, the Great White Throne judgment.

Lightnings, voices, and thunders were the solemn announcement in the beginning of the Great Tribulation that judgment was impending. "And out of the throne proceeded lightnings and thunderings and voices: and there were seven lamps of fire burning before the throne, which are the seven Spirits of God" (Rev. 4:5). Now again at the conclusion of the Tribulation are voices and thunders and lightnings.

"There was a great earthquake, such as was not since men were upon the earth." The Word of God makes it very clear that here at the end of the Great Tribulation period there is to be a horrendous earthquake which probably will shake the entire world.

> **And the great city was divided into three parts, and the cities of the nations fell: and great Babylon came in remembrance before God, to give unto her the cup of the wine of the fierceness of his wrath.**
>
> **And every island fled away, and the mountains were not found.**
>
> **And there fell upon men a great hail out of heaven, every stone about the weight of a talent: and men blasphemed God because of the plague of the hail; for the plague thereof was exceeding great [Rev. 16:19–21].**

And the great city became (divided) into three parts, and the cities of the nations fell: and Babylon the great was

remembered before God, to give to her the cup of the
wine of the indignation of His wrath. And every island
fled away, and mountains were not found. And great
hail, as it were a talent weight, comes down out of heaven
upon men: and men blasphemed God because of the
plagues of the hail; for the plague thereof is exceeding
great.

This concludes the Great Tribulation period. There is a great earthquake, and it divides the "great city," which is Jerusalem. The earthquake divides this city into three parts. Although the center of the earthquake is in Jerusalem, it is not confined to Jerusalem, because we are told that "the cities of the nations fell." This tells us something of the extent and the vast destruction of the earthquake.

"Babylon" is mentioned specifically again. It was mentioned in chapter 14, verse 8, which says, "And there followed another angel, saying, Babylon is fallen, is fallen, that great city, because she made all nations drink of the wine of the wrath of her fornication." The next two chapters give us the details concerning Babylon.

"Every island fled away" reveals that even the islands are shifted from one place to another by the earthquake.

The final act of judgment is the hailstorm. The size of the hailstones is enormous—"a talent weight." The Greek talent was fifty-six pounds, and the Jewish talent was one hundred fourteen pounds. In Texas I can remember seeing hailstones as big as baseballs, but this beats the Texas story altogether. A very interesting hailstorm is recorded during the time of Joshua: "And it came to pass, as they fled from before Israel, and were in the going down to Beth-horon, that the LORD cast down great stones from heaven upon them unto Azekah, and they died: they were more which died with hailstones than they whom the children of Israel slew with the sword" (Josh. 10:11).

According to the historian Josephus, the Roman catapults threw stones the weight of a talent, into Jerusalem in A.D. 70 when Titus leveled the city.

The marvelous hailstorm ends the Great Tribulation period.

CHAPTER 17

THEME: The apostate church in the Great Tribulation

In chapters 17—18 we see the judgment of the two Babylons. We will first see the apostate church in the Great Tribulation in chapter 17, and then we will see not only religious Babylon but also commercial Babylon in chapter 18.

So many great issues are brought to a crisis in the Great Tribulation that it is difficult to keep them separated, and many fine expositors disagree on details. We have already noted this as we have gone through this Book of Revelation. Although we agree with the *system* of interpretation, we do disagree on details.

This fact should not be disturbing to believers, as many details will not be clarified until the world enters the Great Tribulation period and actually faces the climax to each crisis.

This is especially evident relative to the two Babylons in chapters 17—18. The questions are: "Are there two Babylons, and are they in two different geographical locations? Are they representative of two systems? Are they two literal cities, or are they the same?" The answers to these questions will become more apparent as our redemption draws near. It appears at the present time, in my judgment, that two distinct cities are in view.

Here in chapter 17 it is mystery Babylon, the cosmic church, the apostate church. The church of Thyatira, described in chapter 2, verses 18–29, which permitted Jezebel to teach, will become the apostate church of the Great Tribulation. It will attain the goal of the present-day apostates of all the great systems of the world: Romanism, Protestantism, pagan religions, cults and "isms." Even in our so-called independent Bible churches there will be those who are not believers, and during the Tribulation they will join this great organization that may call itself a church but is not. The Bible calls it a harlot. There couldn't be a worse label than that! This is ecumenical ecclesiasticism of the one-world church. The location of this system could be in Rome. Rome, the city built on seven hills, is probably the city in mind here. However, Geneva, where the World Council of Churches has its headquarters, is also included, and other places, such as Los Angeles—if I know Los Angeles, and I think I do—can also make a healthy contribution to it!

It is called *mystery* Babylon because of its origin. At the Tower of Babel man attempted to rally against God. Under Nimrod, Babylon became the origin of all false religion. Now the dream of Nimrod will be realized in the first half of the Great Tribulation period, for the cosmic church dominates the wild Beast. The church that should have been the bride of Christ is a harlot here. This church is guilty of spiritual fornication, selling herself to the world for hire. This is the church that says, "I am rich and increased with goods, and I have need of nothing."

Looking back at the study of the seven churches, in chapters 3—4 of the Book of Revelation, I pointed out that the church in Philadelphia represented the church that would be raptured before the time of the Tribulation period. He said to that church, "I also will keep thee from the hour of temptation" (Rev. 3:10). That "hour" is the Great Tribulation, and we have been in that "hour" a long time in our study of this Book of Revelation.

The true church will not go through the Great Tribulation; it will be raptured before the Tribulation begins. Let's be specific: who will be raptured? Not certain denominations and not just individual churches, but *His* church, a collective term meaning all true believers, those who are in *Christ*. That is the group that will be taken out at the Rapture, and the rest of the church members will be left here on this earth to go through the Great Tribulation. As Dr. George Gill used to say, some churches will meet the Sunday after the Rapture and will not miss a member. But let's clearly understand that they are not true believers. They are not part of the church of the Lord Jesus Christ. He never calls them His church; He calls it a *harlot!* It is a pseudo-religious system, which controls the wild Beast during the first half of the Great Tribulation, yet it is hated by him. During the last half of the Tribulation, the Beast destroys the harlot in order to set up his own religion. J. Dwight Pentecost in his book, *Things To Come* (p. 368), gives this comment concerning the harlot system:

> The Beast, who was dominated by the harlot system (Rev. 17:3), rises against her and destroys her and her system completely. Without doubt the harlot system was in competition with the religious worship of the Beast, promoted by the False Prophet, and her destruction is brought about so that the Beast may be the sole object of false worship as he claims to be God.

Babylon is to be rebuilt, as we have seen in Isaiah and Jeremiah, and here in chapters 17—18 we see it destroyed. Ecclesiastical Babylon will be destroyed by the wild Beast.

Ecclesiastical Babylon is destroyed by the wild Beast.

Commercial Babylon is destroyed by the return of Christ.

Ecclesiastical Babylon is hated by the Beast.

Commercial Babylon is loved by the world.

Ecclesiastical Babylon is destroyed at the *beginning* of the last three and one-half years of the Great Tribulation.

Commercial Babylon is destroyed at the *end* of the last three and one-half years of the Great Tribulation—that is, at the very end. Zechariah 5:5-11 also has something interesting to say in this connection.

GREAT HARLOT RIDING THE WILD BEAST

I do not have words to describe how frightful this picture is. The harlot is the false church, as we have said, And the wild Beast is the restored Roman Empire, which will be brought back together by Antichrist with the assistance, I believe, of the false church.

> **And there came one of the seven angels which had the seven vials, and talked with me, saying unto me, Come hither; I will shew unto thee the judgment of the great whore that sitteth upon many waters:**

> **With whom the kings of the earth have committed forni-
> cation, and the inhabitants of the earth have been made
> drunk with the wine of her fornication [Rev. 17:1–2].**

As usual, I'll give my own literal translation of the Greek text throughout the chapter.

> *And there came one of the seven (7) angels that had the
> seven (7) bowls, and spake with me, saying, Come hither,
> I will show thee the judgment of the great harlot that sit-
> teth upon many waters; with whom the kings of the earth
> committed fornication, and they that dwell in the earth
> were made drunken with the wine of her fornication.*

"The great harlot" is that part of the church that will remain after the
true church has been raptured. It will be composed of those who have
never trusted Christ as Savior; they have never been in the body of
Christ. This is the group that enters the Great Tribulation.

We are told certain things about her. She "sitteth upon many waters." According to verse 15, which we will see later, the "waters" refer
to great masses of people and nations. The harlot will pretty much
control the world.

"The kings of the earth committed fornication" show that there is
an unholy alliance between church and state during that period.

My friend, the movement in our day of bringing all religions together certainly falls into the pattern of this false church which is to
appear—and Scripture doesn't even dignify it by the name of church,
although I am sure it will call itself that. I believe that this movement
is more dangerous to our own country than is any foreign political
system and that it is more dangerous than the so-called new morality. I
believe that it is more dangerous than any other movement. It will
become a power-bloc that will dazzle the unthinking mob. It will
bring the world under the influence of the wild Beast out of the sea
and the wild Beast out of the earth. They will use the apostate church
to control the masses, and the church will yield to this arrangement
for political preferment and power.

You see, when you reject the genuine, you are wide open for the spurious. Paul wrote to the Thessalonians that when someone rejects the love of the truth that they might be saved, they will believe the big lie.

"The judgment of the great harlot." God's cup of judgment will be pressed to the lips of the harlot. And who is going to destroy her? The Beast himself will destroy her. You see, the Antichrist and the False Prophet will not want her around after she has served their purpose. Antichrist wants to be worshiped, and he doesn't want any competition from the church.

> **So he carried me away in the spirit into the wilderness: and I saw a woman sit upon a scarlet coloured beast, full of names of blasphemy, having seven heads and ten horns [Rev. 17:3].**
>
> *And he carried me away in the Spirit into a wilderness; and I saw a woman sitting upon a scarlet-colored wild beast, full of names of blasphemy, having seven heads and ten horns.*

"He carried me away in the Spirit into a wilderness." Remember that John was on the Isle of Patmos in the Spirit for the vision of the glorified Christ and His message to the churches. At that time John was caught up to heaven. From then on the scene shifts from heaven to earth. However, here we are told again that John was in the Spirit. Did he need a fresh anointing of the Spirit for this vision? I rather think so. Is the wilderness literal? Remember that this chapter is a vision where symbols are used. Around both Babylon and Rome there is a literal wilderness. This is a matter of recorded history. Babylon was to become a wilderness, and in this connection read Isaiah 47—48 and Jeremiah 50—51. Outside of Rome the wilderness is called the *campagna*. I believe that the wilderness mentioned in this verse is literal but also that it is a sign of the chaotic condition of the world brought about by the religious confusion of Babylon.

John saw a woman "sitting upon a scarlet-colored wild beast."

This is a frightful and frightening scene. The wild Beast has previously been identified as the Antichrist ruling over the restored Roman Empire. The woman is identified for us in verse 18: "And the woman which thou sawest is that great city, which reigneth over the kings of the earth." The woman is a city, and the city is Rome, the religious capital of the world. She is religious Rome, which at that time will have inherited all the religions of the world. You see, all true believers will have left the world scene at the time of the Rapture. This includes *all* true believers, and I have discovered that there are many true believers in Romanism and in liberal churches and even in some very weird religious systems. All genuine believers, regardless of where they have gone to church, will be raptured. This will leave a church on earth that is totally apostate. Rather than being "the bride of Christ," God calls it a harlot.

The city is further identified in verse 9: "And here is the mind which hath wisdom. The seven heads are seven mountains, on which the woman sitteth." Rome was the city set on seven hills and was known as such to both pagan and Christian writers. Horace wrote, "The gods, who look with favour on the seven hills. . . ." Ovid added, "But Rome looks around on the whole globe from her seven mountains, the seat of empire and abode of the gods." Augustine wrote, "Babylon is a former Rome, and Rome is a later Babylon." In these verses the city of Rome is assuredly in view. The woman, the harlot, represents a religious system that will be revealed during the first part of the Great Tribulation period after the true church has been removed from the earth. And this religious system, as the symbol given to us indicates, dominates and rides the Roman Empire at the beginning of the Great Tribulation period.

"Full of names of blasphemy" reveals how far religion will have departed from the living Christ.

And the woman was arrayed in purple and scarlet colour, and decked with gold and precious stones and pearls, having a golden cup in her hand full of abominations and filthiness of her fornication:

And upon her forehead was a name written, MYSTERY, BABYLON THE GREAT, THE MOTHER OF HARLOTS AND ABOMINATIONS OF THE EARTH [Rev. 17:4–5].

And the woman was clothed in purple and scarlet, and gilded with gold, and precious stone and pearls, having in her hand a golden cup full of abominations, even the unclean things of her fornication, and upon her forehead a name written MYSTERY, BABYLON THE GREAT, THE MOTHER OF THE HARLOTS AND OF THE ABOMINA-TIONS OF THE EARTH.

"Clothed in purple and scarlet." Purple was the predominant color of Roman imperialism. Every senator and consul wore a purple stripe as a badge of his position, and the emperor's robes were purple. Scarlet is the color adopted by Roman Catholicism.

"Gilded with gold" shows the beauty of the outward display, but, like the Pharisees, it is within "full of dead men's bones and of all uncleanness."

"Precious stones and pearls" are pretty cold, though they may be genuine, and are a sordid imitation of genuine heartfelt religion. The Lord Jesus said, "Woe unto you, scribes and Pharisees, hypocrites! for ye make clean the outside of the cup and of the platter, but within they are full of extortion and excess" (Matt. 23:25).

"A golden cup full of abominations" is the religious intoxication of the anti-church (not Antichrist) and a pseudoreligion, counterfeit Christianity, a fake and false gospel, and a sham and spurious system. This is the cup which makes the world drunk. "Babylon hath been a golden cup in the LORD's hand, that made all the earth drunken: the nations have drunken of her wine; therefore the nations are mad" (Jer. 51:7).

"Upon her forehead a name written" is a startling revelation of the character of this woman. She does not wear a crown but rather the mark of her profession. It is of interest to see that Seneca, in addressing a wanton priestess, said, "Thy name hung from thy forehead." "MYSTERY, BABYLON THE GREAT, THE MOTHER OF THE HAR-

LOTS AND OF THE ABOMINATIONS OF THE EARTH" is the disgraceful title for the "church" which should belong to Christ as a bride.

Now I know that we live in a day of changing morality, but I am a little old-fashioned, and I still think that the Word of God is right in its values. I think that the finest thing in the world is a woman and that God has made her that way. When she marries, she is brought into a relationship in which she can give to a man that which puts him in orbit. It is my firm conviction that the thing our civilization has done for a woman has not been to liberate her but to enslave her so that she has become more of a sex symbol than ever before. Instead of taking her rightful place where she can lift a man to the heights, she is characterized as the one who pulls him down to the depths. And the lowest picture you can have is that of a harlot. You may not like it, but that is how the Word of God sees it.

"MYSTERY BABYLON." The true church is a mystery in that it was not revealed in the Old Testament (see Eph. 3:1–9). The anti-church, designated here as a harlot, is a mystery in that it was not revealed until John wrote Revelation 17. Let me say again that when the true church left the earth at the time of the Rapture, the phonies, those who were only church members, entered the Great Tribulation period, and the system continued—not now a church, but a harlot. Paul had written of the mystery of iniquity: "For the mystery of iniquity doth already work: only he who now hinders will hinder until he be taken out of the way" (2 Thess. 2:7). The anti-church is the antithesis of the true church, which is the virgin bride of Christ, and it is the consummation of the working of "the mystery of iniquity." It is "MYSTERY BABYLON" because it is given this designation just as Jerusalem is called Sodom.

Babylon is the fountainhead for all false religion; therefore she is "THE MOTHER OF THE HARLOTS AND OF THE ABOMINATIONS OF THE EARTH." This is, by far, Scripture's more expressive and vivid picture of awful and abominable sin. Sex and false religions are related, you may be sure of that. I believe that many young people are really missing it in marriage when they do not stand at the marriage altar in the presence of God presenting themselves to each other, having kept their bodies for the marriage. That was God's ideal and still is.

Have you noticed that this "MYSTERY BABYLON" is called the "MOTHER OF THE HARLOTS"? The mother of harlots—not singular but plural. In our day the ecumenical church has faced a lot of problems. It seems that they have recognized psychological differences in people and that it is impossible to water down theologies and practices to suit everyone. So each group will come into this great world ecumenical system but retain some of its pecularities. For example, those who want to immerse will immerse. Those who want to sprinkle will sprinkle. Those who want elaborate ritual will have it, and those who want no ritual will have that. You see, there is going to be more than the mother harlot—there will be a whole lot of harlots, a regular brothel.

> **And I saw the woman drunken with the blood of the saints, and with the blood of the martyrs of Jesus: and when I saw her, I wondered with great admiration.**
>
> **And the angel said unto me, Wherefore didst thou marvel? I will tell thee the mystery of the woman, and of the beast that carrieth her, which hath the seven heads and ten horns [Rev. 17:6–7].**
>
> *And I saw the woman drunken with the blood of the saints, and with the blood of the martyrs of Jesus. And when I saw her, I wondered with a great wonder. And the angel said unto me, Wherefore didst thou wonder? I will tell thee the mystery of the woman, and of the wild beast that is carrying her, which hath the seven heads and ten horns.*

"Drunken with the blood of the saints." The harlot not only makes others drunk, but she is intoxicated by her acts of persecution. While it is true that the church will not go through the Great Tribulation, as we near the end of this age of grace, believers can expect some tribulation. It is my experience and that of other Christian leaders that today it is becoming increasingly difficult to stand for the Word of God and for the things of Christ.

"The saints" probably refers to Old Testament saints, and "the martyrs of Jesus" refers to New Testament saints. This indicates that "BABYLON" is more than just Romanism. Rather, it is an amalgam of all religions. All true believers were caught up at the Rapture, and Babylon is the residue of what is left.

Babylon is a composite religious system which includes Protestantism, Romanism, cults—the whole lot which was not raptured, you see. It is confusion compounded and is the fountainhead of all religious error and idolatry. Babylon in the Old Testament persecuted God's people and was the enemy of God. It was Babylon that put the three Hebrew boys in the fiery furnace because they would not worship an image.

When John saw the vision of the woman, he says that he "wondered with a great wonder." This is the first time that John has had his mind boggled. We have had our minds boggled before, but this really throws John. The angel asks why he should wonder when he (the angel) was present to explain the mystery of the woman.

The emphasis here is on the Roman Empire aspect of the wild beast rather than on the Antichrist aspect. We should note that.

> **The beast that thou sawest was, and is not; and shall ascend out of the bottomless pit, and go into perdition: and they that dwell on the earth shall wonder, whose names were not written in the book of life from the foundation of the world, when they behold the beast that was, and is not, and yet is.**

> **And here is the mind which hath wisdom. The seven heads are seven mountains, on which the woman sitteth.**

> **And there are seven kings: five are fallen, and one is, and the other is not yet come; and when he cometh, he must continue a short space [Rev. 17:8–10].**

The wild beast which thou sawest was and is not; and is about to come up out of the abyss, and to go (goeth) into perdition. And those dwelling on the earth shall wonder, whose names are not written upon the book of life from the foundation of the world (cosmos), when they behold the wild beast because it was, and is not, and shall come (be present). Here is the mind having wisdom. The seven heads are seven mountains on which the woman sitteth. And there are seven kings; the five have fallen (fell), the one is, the other is not yet come; and when he cometh, he must continue a little while.

The wild beast "was" speaks of the past history of the Roman Empire. "Is not" refers to the present condition of the fragmented Empire. The Roman Empire is not dead. It has fallen apart into the nations of Europe today. "Is about to come up out of the abyss" speaks of the reactivation of the Roman Empire by Satan.

As I have indicated before, many have attempted to put the Roman Empire back together again but have never been successful. Charlemagne tried it, Napoleon tried it, Hitler tried it, Mussolini tried it, and at the time I am writing this, the United Nations is trying it, but they, too, are failing. The wild Beast, who is the Antichrist, will be the one who puts the Roman Empire back together again.

"Shall . . . go into perdition" speaks of the destruction of the Roman Empire by the coming of Christ. The reappearance of the Roman Empire in its great power will win the admiration of the peoples of the world who are not redeemed. They will respect and worship the Antichrist for his brilliant *coup d'etat.* God's saints will have the mind of the Spirit and will understand and not be spiritually stupid: "But ye have an unction from the Holy One, and ye know all things. . . . But the anointing which ye have received of him abideth in you, and ye need not that any man teach you: but as the same anointing teacheth you of all things, and is truth, and is no lie, and even as it hath taught you, ye shall abide in him" (1 John 2:20, 27).

"And there are seven kings" is taken by some (including Newell and Govett, who are excellent commentators on Revelation) to mean individual rulers. Govett gives the following list:

1. Julius Caesar—assassinated
2. Tiberius—poisoned or smothered
3. Caligula—assassinated
4. Claudius—poisoned
5. Nero—committed suicide

"The one is" refers to Domitian who was living in John's day, who was also assassinated.

"The other is not yet come" refers to the Antichrist. Other expositors (as Scofield and Walter Scott) consider these seven as the different forms of government through which Rome passed. These are listed as kings, consuls, dictators, decemvirs, and military tribunes. "The one is" refers to the sixth or imperial form of government set up by Julius Caesar and under which John was banished by Domitian. The seventh and last, though it has not yet appeared, will be satanic in form.

Regardless of the interpretation adopted, the end in view is the same—the Antichrist rules over the reactivated Roman Empire.

> **And the beast that was, and is not, even he is the eighth, and is of the seven, and goeth into perdition.**
>
> **And the ten horns which thou sawest are ten kings, which have received no kingdom as yet; but receive power as kings one hour with the beast.**
>
> **These have one mind, and shall give their power and strength unto the beast.**
>
> **These shall make war with the Lamb, and the Lamb shall overcome them: for he is Lord of lords, and King of kings: and they that are with him are called, and chosen, and faithful [Rev. 17:11–14].**
>
> *And the beast that was, and is not, is himself also an eighth, and is of the seven, and is going into perdition. And the ten horns that thou sawest are ten kings, who (of the kind which) have received no kingdom as yet; but*

> they receive authority as kings, with the wild beast, for
> one hour. These have one mind, and they give (over) their
> power and authority unto the beast. These shall war with
> the Lamb, and the Lamb shall overcome them, for He is
> Lord of lords, and King of kings; and those with Him
> (shall overcome), called and chosen and faithful.

At times the wild beast signifies, generally, the Roman Empire, but also it signifies the last or eighth head; that is, the individual emperor who is Antichrist. Now here the Antichrist is designated. He is the "little horn" in the vision that God gave to the prophet Daniel. The "little horn" puts down three other horns—that is, three kings—when he comes to power. "I considered the horns, and, and, behold, there came up among them another little horn, before whom there were three of the first horns plucked up by the roots: and, behold, in this horn were eyes like the eyes of man, and a mouth speaking great things. . . . And the ten horns out of this kingdom are ten kings that shall arise: and another shall rise after them; and he shall be diverse from the first, and he shall subdue three kings" (Dan. 7:8, 24). In my book, *Delving Through Daniel*, I go into detail on this "little horn."

"The beast that was" refers to the past history of the Roman Empire under the emperors.

"And is not" refers to the end of Imperial Rome with its global empire, which came to an end sometime between the third and fifth centuries.

"Is himself also an eighth, and is of the seven" identifies the Antichrist with the return to the imperial form of the restored Roman Empire. He is the "little horn" of Daniel, chapter 7. He is not one of the ten horns, but he is separate from them. He is an eighth head in this seven, yet he is one of the seven since he restores the last form of government to Rome. Now that will confuse you, I know, but that is exactly what is being said here in Revelation.

"The ten horns" are the same as the ten horns of Daniel 7:7. These ten kings will reign with the Antichrist but will be subservient to him. They willingly or unwillingly give over their authority to the Antichrist and become his puppets.

And he saith unto me, The waters which thou sawest, where the whore sitteth, are peoples, and multitudes, and nations, and tongues.

And the ten horns which thou sawest upon the beast, these shall hate the whore, and shall make her desolate and naked, and shall eat her flesh, and burn her with fire.

For God hath put in their hearts to fulfil his will, and to agree, and give their kingdom unto the beast, until the words of God shall be fulfilled.

And the woman which thou sawest is that great city, which reigneth over the kings of the earth [Rev. 17:15–18].

And he saith to me, The waters which thou sawest where the harlot sitteth, are peoples, and multitudes (mobs), and nations, and tongues. And the ten horns which thou sawest, and the beast, these shall hate the harlot, and shall make her desolated and naked, and shall eat her flesh, and shall burn her (down) with fire. For God did put into their hearts to do His mind, and to come to one mind, and to give their kingdom unto the beast, until the words of God shall be fulfilled. And the woman whom thou sawest is the great city, which hath a kingdom over the kings of the earth.

"The waters" are explained to be the many ethnological groups as well as the nations of the world. This figure is in harmony with that used in the Old Testament. You can check that out with Isaiah 8:7 and Psalm 18. The position of the harlot reveals that she is ruling over them for only a brief time.

"The ten horns" are ten kings (as told us in verse 12) who rule over the different divisions of the Roman Empire. They in turn give over to the Beast their kingdoms. This solidifies the Roman Empire and enables the Beast to lift himself up as a world dictator.

For a time the Beast (Antichrist) is willing to share his place of exaltation with the harlot, since she has also sought to advance his cause while dividing his glory. This he hates, and the ten kings are one with him in this. The Antichrist not only breaks his covenant with Israel, but he also breaks his relationship with the apostate church. This hatred against the apostate church is so violent that the reaction is described as the cannibalistic picking of her bones, then burning them with fire! This great hatred destroys the false church. This is what happens to the false church. It has no victory. It never comes into the presence of Christ. It is not raptured. Finally it is destroyed by the Antichrist.

In doing this the Antichrist and his ten allies are fulfilling the Word of God and carrying out His will as did the Assyrian (as predicted in Isaiah 10:5–19) and just as surely as Caesar Augustus did when he signed the tax bill that moved Mary and Joseph down to Bethlehem so Scripture could be fulfilled.

By eliminating the apostate church, the way is cleared for the worship of Antichrist, as advocated by the False Prophet.

"The woman" is a religious system, as we have seen. Also, I believe she is further identified as a city, the city of Rome.

This is the frightful but just end of the apostate church. However, it does not improve the situation. Rather it introduces the darkest period for religion in the history of the world. The reign and religion of Antichrist is the darkest hour earth will know, and yet it is the inevitable end of the distrust which began in the Garden of Eden when man failed to believe God. It was given new impetus at the Tower of Babel, which was a rallying place for those against God. And finally it climaxed in the crucifixion of Jesus Christ when man rejected the One who is the Way, the Truth, and the Life. Having rejected the truth, the only alternative left for man is to believe the big lie, the strong delusion. History will culminate in the catastrophic coming of Christ to this earth, as we shall see in chapter 19. This is the just retribution of error and evil.

My friend, you as a Christian should have thankfulness in your heart, knowing you will be spared from the Great Tribulation, but also you should have a real concern for your loved ones who may be facing this frightful period that lies ahead.

CHAPTER 18

THEME: Political and commercial Babylon judged

In the chapter before us we see the judgment of commercial Babylon and the reaction of both earth and heaven to it.

In chapters 17—18 two Babylons are brought before us. The Babylon of chapter 17 is ecclesiastical. The Babylon of chapter 18 is economic. The first is religious—the apostate church which entered the Great Tribulation period. The second is political and commercial. The commercial center is *loved* by the kings of the earth; and the apostate church is *hated* by the kings of the earth, as we saw in chapter 17. The apostate church is destroyed by the kings of the earth. When Christ returns, political Babylon will be destroyed by the judgment of God. Obviously, mystery Babylon, the apostate church, is destroyed first in the midst of the Great Tribulation, while commercial Babylon will be destroyed at the second coming of Christ. These two Babylons are not one and the same city. I personally believe that mystery Babylon is Rome and that, when it goes down in the midst of the Great Tribulation, the religious center shifts to Jerusalem because it is at Jerusalem that the False Prophet will put up his image of the Antichrist to be worshiped. Commercial Babylon is ancient Babylon, rebuilt as the commercial capital of the world. This city is the final capital of the political power of the Beast.

A few years ago it seemed rather farfetched that the power could reach back into the Mideast, but since then we have experienced a shortage of energy, and when they cut off the oil supply, the whole world feels it. They wield tremendous power. The wealth of the world is moving into that particular area because of the price of oil. It could well become the great commercial capital of the world. And this great commercial center, which will be Babylon rebuilt, will be destroyed at the second coming of Christ.

Sometime ago a Jew challenged the Israeli minister of tourism by saying, "How does it come about that all the countries surrounding Israel have oil, but Israel doesn't?" His reply was this: "God gave the Arabs oil and the Jews the Bible. Do you want to exchange with them? God forbid. The oil will run out quick enough, but the Bible will last forever."

There had been some disagreement among conservative expositors about whether or not ancient Babylon will be rebuilt. Candidly, for many years I took the position that it would not be rebuilt. However, I believe now that it will be rebuilt. Isaiah 13:19–22 speaks of the fact that ancient Babylon is to be rebuilt and destroyed, and this destruction is what is mentioned in chapter 18 of Revelation, which is before us. Actually, I don't think it could be rebuilt on the same spot because the Euphrates River has moved about fourteen miles from the ancient city.

There are two views of the destruction of Babylon which are diametrically opposed to each other. The viewpoint and perspective are highly important. (1) The reaction of men of business and politics is one of great anguish. To them it is the depth of tragedy. It means the total bankruptcy of big business. (2) The second reaction is that of heaven. It is one of joy that the holiness and justice of God is vindicated. It means the end of man's sinful career on earth. This will bring to an end the Great Tribulation period.

ANNOUNCEMENT AND FALL OF COMMERCIAL AND POLITICAL BABYLON

Chapter 18 begins with "another angel" who comes down from heaven with a message.

And after these things I saw another angel come down from heaven, having great power; and the earth was lightened with his glory [Rev. 18:1].

As usual, I'll give my literal translation of the Greek text throughout this chapter.

After these things I saw another angel coming down out of heaven, having great authority; and the earth was lightened with his glory.

Again we have this very interesting statement, "after these things" (Gr.: *meta tauta*). After what things? After the series of sevens and after the judgment of religious Babylon come these things. Progress has definitely been made—through the seven seals, the seven trumpets, the seven personages, and the seven bowls of wrath—and we are advancing to the end of the Great Tribulation. In fact, this brings us to the end of the Great Tribulation.

John says, "I saw." He is still a spectator. He saw "another angel," which takes us back to chapter 14 where a series of six angels is mentioned, each with the sole identification of "another angel." This angel is a divine, supernatural messenger of God, but faceless and nameless. He has *great authority* (power), which indicates that he has a superior rank to the other "another angel," and he is bringing an important message.

"The earth was lightened with his glory" seems to further signify the prestige of this angel (cf. Ezek. 43:2).

And he cried mightily with a strong voice, saying, Babylon the great is fallen, is fallen, and is become the habitation of devils, and the hold of every foul spirit, and a cage of every unclean and hateful bird [Rev. 18:2].

And he shouted with a mighty voice, saying, Fell, fell is Babylon the great, and became a habitation of demons, and a prison (hold, cage) of every unclean spirit, and a prison (hold, cage) of every unclean and hated bird.

The preliminary announcement of the fall of Babylon was made in Revelation 14:8: "And there followed another angel, saying, Babylon is fallen, is fallen, that great city, because she made all nations drink of the wine of the wrath of her fornication." The angel here is greater in authority than the one who made that first announcement.

In the words, "Fell, fell is Babylon . . . and became," the tense in the Greek is prophetic aorist which speaks of coming events as if they have already transpired. When God says something is going to happen, you can speak about it as though it had already happened, because it is going to happen. It is just that sure. In God's plan and program it is just as though it had already taken place because He knows the end from the beginning. Babylon, this great commercial center of the world, is going to be destroyed.

"A habitation of demons, and a cage of every unclean spirit, and a cage of every unclean and hated bird." This indicates that Babylon is where demons of the spirit world and unclean birds of the physical world will be incarcerated during the Millennium. The prophets Isaiah and Jeremiah confirm this (see Isa. 13:19–22; Jer. 50:38–40). These prophecies find a final fulfillment in the destruction of literal Babylon here in Revelation 18. If this is true, there is no prophecy which forbids Babylon from being rebuilt. Babylon is the headquarters of demons and has been the place of rebellion down through the years.

> **For all nations have drunk of the wine of the wrath of her fornication, and the kings of the earth have committed fornication with her, and the merchants of the earth are waxed rich through the abundance of her delicacies [Rev. 18:3].**

> *For by the wine of the wrath of her fornication all the nations have drunk (or are fallen); and the kings of the earth committed fornication with her, and the merchants of the earth waxed rich by the power of her wantonness.*

"Have drunk" (or are fallen) are the two permitted renderings—both have good manuscript authority. Both are true. The normal rendering is "have drunk." This is God's judgment on big business which denies God's authority. This is the unholy alliance of government and business. We have seen some of this in our day and, frankly, it smells to high heaven.

The word for merchants means "those who travel." It is not those who produce goods or manufacture goods, but those who are brokers, engaging in business for a big profit. Business is a sacred cow that nothing must harm or hinder. This is true today, of course. Man uses business as the biggest excuse for having no time for God, yet these same men must finally stand before God. God will judge godless commercialism. Big business is in for it, I can assure you of that. In fact, it has had a rough time in our day.

And I heard another voice from heaven, saying, Come out of her, my people, that ye be not partakers of her sins, and that ye receive not of her plagues [Rev. 18:4].

And I heard another voice out of heaven, saying, Come forth out of her, my people, that ye have no fellowship with her sins, and that ye receive not of her plagues.

This verse reveals that God's people are going to be in the world to the very end (it is not speaking of the church which has already been removed before the Great Tribulation began), but God will have His people on earth during the Tribulation. The question has always been: Will they be able to make it through? That is, will they remain faithful to Christ? Yes, they do make it through. Remember that God started with 144,000, and the number that will make it through the Tribulation is 144,000. This is like the parable the Lord Jesus told about the shepherd who started out with one hundred sheep and one of them got away. But he didn't end up with ninety-nine; he ended up with one hundred, because he went out and got that little sheep that was lost.

The One who is speaking in this verse is none other than the Son of God, and He is calling His people out of Babylon before the judgment comes. It is a physical separation with a corollary in the experience of Lot in Sodom. As Lot was warned to get out of Sodom to escape the deluge of fire (see Gen. 19), so these people of God are warned. God's Word tells us, "When thou art in tribulation, and all these things are come upon thee, even in the latter days, if thou turn to the LORD thy God, and shalt be obedient unto his voice; (For the LORD thy God is a merciful God;) he will not forsake thee, neither destroy thee, nor forget the covenant of thy fathers which he sware unto them" (Deut. 4:30–31).

Such was also God's warning to Israel in Jeremiah 51:5–6, 45 and in Isaiah 48:20. The warning is twofold: (1) They are to have no fellowship with the sins of Babylon and (2) they are to flee before judgment falls.

I think this has a pertinent application for us today. It should be a warning to us, not that God will fail to save His own from this hour, but that He wants us to be separate, not indulging the old nature, but walking by the Spirit. If we will not deal with sin in our own lives here and now by confessing and forsaking it, He will deal with it. Either He will judge sin now, or it will meet us at the judgment seat of Christ. God gives us the opportunity of judging our sin today: "For if we would judge ourselves, we should not be judged. But when we are judged, we are chastened of the Lord, that we should not be condemned with the world" (1 Cor. 11:31–32).

How can we judge our own sin? First John 1:9 has the answer: "If we confess our sins, he is faithful and just to forgive us our sins, and to cleanse us from all unrighteousness." To "confess" means to say the same thing that God says about it. It means to take God's viewpoint and say, "God, I agree with You. What I did was sin." It is so easy to make excuses for our own sin. We say that ours is not really sin—of course, if our neighbors do it, it is sin. But until you and I are willing to call our sin sin, we haven't confessed it at all. If we refuse to judge ourselves, we will be judged at the judgment seat of Christ. The sins of some folk will not be settled until they stand before the judgment seat of Christ. I hope to get all of my accounts straightened out down here. Just because God may not take us to the woodshed immediately does not mean that He is letting us get by without punishment. He doesn't spank the Devil's children, but if you are His child, judgment will come to you.

For her sins have reached unto heaven, and God hath remembered her iniquities [Rev. 18:5].

Babylon has a long history of accumulated sins, and God has the record. It is one of the oldest cities in the history of mankind and is probably mentioned more than any other city in the Bible, with the exception of Jerusalem. Finally judgment breaks like a flood upon this city and its system. The judgment of God may be delayed, but it is sure. It may seem to us that the unbeliever is getting by with sin, but God's judgment is coming.

> **Reward her even as she rewarded you, and double unto her double according to her works: in the cup which she hath filled fill to her double [Rev. 18:6].**

> *Render unto her even as she also rendered, and double unto her the double according to her works; in the cup which she mingled, mingle unto her double.*

This is poetic justice (see Obad. 15). The cup of iniquity is being filled to the brim; when the last drop is poured in, it is pressed to the lips of those who committed iniquity. My friend, this is *just*—read Psalm 137. God is right and just in what He does.

> **How much she hath glorified herself, and lived deliciously, so much torment and sorrow give her: for she saith in her heart, I sit a queen, and am no widow, and shall see no sorrow [Rev. 18:7].**

> *How much soever she glorified herself, and waxed wanton (lived in luxury), so much give her of torment and mourning; for she saith in her heart, I sit a queen, and am no widow, and shall in no wise see mourning.*

You see, the prosperity of Babylon blinded her to the judgment of God. Trading was active on the stock market, and everyone bought blue chip issues right up to the moment of judgment. Luxury, arrogance, pride, sin, and self-deception characterized the spirit of this godless city. World peace was in sight, and optimism was the spirit of the day. Only the prophets of gloom issued a warning, and they were classified as "squares," as was Noah (and as Vernon McGee is today).

> **Therefore shall her plagues come in one day, death, and mourning, and famine; and she shall be utterly burned with fire: for strong is the Lord God who judgeth her [Rev. 18:8].**

This calls to our attention the suddenness of destruction and that it will be by "fire." So great is her grief that "mourning" is counted a plague along with "death" and "famine." Death, mourning, and famine are the three horsemen who ride roughshod over Babylon. The destruction is total and final. In the Scriptures this is the first city of prominence, but its long, eventful and sinful history ends with the judgment of God upon her.

"For strong is the Lord God who judgeth her." It is God who destroys this city because He alone is able to do it. He does this, we believe, at the return of Christ. Notice this as Isaiah predicts it: "Who is this that cometh from Edom, with dyed garments from Bozrah? this that is glorious in his apparel, travelling in the greatness of his strength? I that speak in righteousness, mighty to save. Wherefore art thou red in thine apparel, and thy garments like him that treadeth in the winevat? I have trodden the winepress alone; and of the people there was none with me: for I will tread them in mine anger, and trample them in my fury; and their blood shall be sprinkled upon my garments, and I will stain all my raiment. For the day of vengeance is in mine heart, and the year of my redeemed is come" (Isa. 63:1–4).

In His second coming Christ is seen coming from Edom with blood-sprinkled garments. It is my belief that He has come by way of Babylon, and He has executed judgment upon that wicked city. We will see Christ's second coming in the following chapter.

Next we will see the reaction to the destruction of this great center. There will be anguish in the world, and we will see who attends her funeral. Also there will be the anticipation of joy in heaven because of the judgment of Babylon. These are the two diametrically opposite viewpoints. It will be bad for one crowd and good for the other crowd.

ANGUISH IN THE WORLD BECAUSE OF
BABYLON'S JUDGMENT

And the kings of the earth, who have committed fornication and lived deliciously with her, shall bewail her,
and lament for her, when they shall see the smoke of her
burning,

Standing afar off for the fear of her torment, saying,
Alas, alas that great city Babylon, that mighty city! for
in one hour is thy judgment come [Rev. 18:9–10].

*And the kings of the earth, who committed fornication
and lived deliciously (in luxury) with her, shall weep
and wail over her, when they look upon the smoke of her
burning, standing afar off for the fear of her torment, saying, Woe, woe, the great city, Babylon, the strong city! for
in one hour is thy judgment come.*

In that day Babylon will dominate and rule the world. The capital of
Antichrist will be Babylon, and he will have the first total dictatorship. The world will become an awful place. In that day everything
will center in Babylon. The stock market will be read from Babylon—
not New York. Babylon instead of Paris will set the styles for the
world. A play, to be successful, will have to be a success in Babylon,
not London. Everything in that city will be in rebellion against almighty God, and it centers in Antichrist.

No one dreamed that this great city would be judged. Yet by the
time the sun goes down, Babylon is nothing but smoldering ruins.
When the news goes out, the world is stunned, and then begins the
wail. The whole world will howl when Babylon goes down. I imagine
that, if you were on the moon, you would have to tune down your
earphones because the howl would be so loud!

In chapter 17 we saw that the kings of the earth hated religious
Babylon and that Antichrist got rid of it in order that he might be
worshiped without any competition in that area of religion. And the
kings of the earth joined in her destruction.

In contrast to this, here in chapter 18 we see that the kings of the earth love commercial Babylon because of the revenue she brought to their coffers. In fact, it is called here fornication—you can't find a better word for it than that! All the lobbyists were in Babylon, not Washington, D.C. They were representing all the great corporations in the world. But the kings desert Babylon like rats leaving a sinking ship; their mourning is both pathetic and contemptible. They eulogize her with panegyrics of praise, but there is a hopelessness in their anguish. They marvel at the sudden destruction of that which they thought was gilt-edged security. The judgment came in the space of one hour, reminding us of the sudden devastation caused by atomic explosions. This is a frightful picture presented to us, and it is the final conflagration and catastrophic judgment that will bring Christ to the earth to set up His Kingdom.

And the merchants of the earth shall weep and mourn over her; for no man buyeth their merchandise any more:

The merchandise of gold, and silver, and precious stones, and of pearls, and fine linen, and purple, and silk, and scarlet, and all thyine wood, and all manner vessels of ivory, and all manner vessels of most precious wood, and of brass, and iron, and marble,

And cinnamon, and odours, and ointments, and frankincense, and wine, and oil, and fine flour, and wheat, and beasts, and sheep, and horses, and chariots, and slaves, and souls of men.

And the fruits that thy soul lusted after are departed from thee, and all things which were dainty and goodly are departed from thee, and thou shalt find them no more at all.

The merchants of these things, which were made rich by her, shall stand afar off for the fear of her torment, weeping and wailing,

> And saying, Alas, alas, that great city, that was clothed
> in fine linen, and purple, and scarlet, and decked with
> gold, and precious stones, and pearls!
>
> For in one hour so great riches is come to nought [Rev.
> 18:11–17a].

As you read these verses, did you feel as if you might be window-shopping down the main street of some of our great cities? In our store windows we see all these things in our day. These are the products of an affluent society, and these things were available to the Roman Empire in John's day. Babylon will make these luxury items necessities, just as we think these items are necessities today. You will not find a cotton dress or a pair of overalls anywhere in this list.

I remember when glazed bitreous terra cotta bathtubs first were introduced in this country. (Incidentally, it was opposed by the doctors in our land. They said that if you took a bath every day, it would shorten your life. They felt a bath once a week or once a month was enough.) In those days the bathtub was a luxury that many folk couldn't afford. But now, when we go to a hotel or motel, my wife looks to see if there is a tub, and I look to see if there is a shower, and generally both are present. We live in a luxury age. Most of what we call necessities are actually luxuries.

Let's look at these items, using my literal translation. We will take them up separately:

"And the merchants of the earth weep and mourn over her, for no man buyeth their merchandise (cargo) any more: merchandise (cargo) of gold, and silver, and precious stones, and pearls." Talk about a depression—they are having one! No one buys their merchandise or cargo anymore. In Babylon there is merchandise of gold and silver, precious stones and pearls. You see, we are in the jewelry department here.

Then we move from the jewelry department to the ladies' ready-to-wear: ". . . and fine linen, and purple, and silk, and scarlet."

Then to the luxury gift department: ". . . and all thyine (citron) wood, and every vessel of ivory, and every vessel made of most precious wood, and of brass, and iron, and marble."

We move on to the spice and cosmetic department: ". . . and cinnamon, and spice (amomum), and odours, and ointment, and frankincense." They have a great deal of spray deodorant, you see—probably the kind that works twenty-four hours a day.

Now we go to the liquor department and the pastry center: "and wine, and oil, and fine flour, and wheat." This is the food of the rich; barley is the food of the poor. The wealthy were eating gourmet food and enjoying luxury until Babylon went down.

We move on to the meat department where you can get porterhouse steaks, lamb chops and filet mignon—"and cattle, and sheep."

The merchandise covers every phase of business. The articles are for a society accustomed to the better things of the material universe. Even men were bought and sold, including their souls. I think this is becoming more and more true today where great corporations have men on the payroll who are bound there almost like slaves. Right now there is many a woman selling her soul. "And merchandise of horses, and chariots, and slaves (bodies), and souls of men."

"The merchants of these things who grew rich by her, shall stand afar off because of the fear of her torment, saying Alas, alas." The Greek word for "alas" doesn't need to be translated to get its meaning. It is *ouai, ouai!* The very sound of the word is a form of wail. The merchants of the earth sit before their TV screens and cry, "Ouai, ouai!" for in one hour wealth so great is laid desolate.

We always have been able to find a parallel in the Old Testament. Do we have anything that corresponds to this in the past? Yes, Ezekiel predicted the judgment of Tyre, the capital of the Phoenicians. Tyre was to the ancient world what New York City is to us today and what Babylon will be to the future (see Ezek. 26—27).

And every shipmaster, and all the company in ships, and sailors, and as many as trade by sea, stood afar off.

And cried when they saw the smoke of her burning, saying, What city is like unto this great city!

And they cast dust on their heads, and cried, weeping and wailing, saying, Alas, alas, that great city, wherein

**were made rich all that had ships in the sea by reason of
her costliness! for in one hour is she made desolate [Rev.
18:17b–19].**

*And every shipmaster and every one that sails anywhere
(traveler) and sailors, and those who live by seafaring
stood afar off. And cried out when they looked upon the
smoke of her burning, saying, What city is like the great
city? And they cast dust upon their heads, and cried,
weeping and mourning, saying, Woe, woe [Gr.: ouai,
ouai], the great city wherein all that had their ships in
the sea were made rich by reason of her costly expendi-
ture! for in one hour is she made desolate.*

The third delegation of mourners is composed of those who are engaged in transportation, the great public carriers. They had become
rich by transporting the merchandise of Babylon, just as the Phoenicians had done in the ancient world. Now there is no more business.
They mourn because of the depression. All went up in smoke in a
moment. They, like the others, marvel at the sudden destruction.

All of this has an application for us. How do *we* see the luxury of
this world? Do we see it as it really is? Can we use it without getting it
into our hearts? How would you feel if the luxuries in your life which
you have come to consider necessities suddenly went up in smoke?

Today we speak about spirituality and spiritual things. Even in our
Christian organizations there is almost an overweening zeal to get
people to give, especially the wealthy people. Recently some wealthy
persons threatened to withdraw their support from my radio ministry
if I did not do a certain thing. I did not listen to their threats. It seems
to me that we have paid too much attention to this world today. The
world is passing away, and the things you see at your fingertips are
also passing away.

The great cities of the world are passing away. Los Angeles is a
wonderful city, and I have enjoyed this city because I have lived in
Southern California for many years, but it is passing away. God is go-

ing to judge Los Angeles. But the question is: Would it break your heart if you saw the things of this world go up in smoke? Or is your heart in heaven, fixed on Christ? It does make a lot of difference.

ANTICIPATION OF JOY IN HEAVEN BECAUSE OF BABYLON'S JUDGMENT

Rejoice over her, thou heaven, and ye holy apostles and prophets; for God hath avenged you on her [Rev. 18:20].

Rejoice over her, thou heaven, and ye saints, and ye apostles, and ye prophets; for God hath judged your judgment on her.

The viewpoint of heaven is entirely different. It is no funeral procession there. Rather, it is the celebration of an anticipated event. The saints prayed for it; the prophets of the Old Testament predicted it. Now all is fulfilled and there is joy because God has exonerated His name. Judgment has come upon these things. Just what is your heart fixed on today? It will make a lot of difference in that day because you will either be with the mourners or you will be with the rejoicers.

And a mighty angel took up a stone like a great millstone, and cast it into the sea, saying, Thus with violence shall that great city Babylon be thrown down, and shall be found no more at all [Rev. 18:21].

And one strong angel took up a stone like a great millstone, and cast it into the sea, saying, Thus with a mighty rush (fall) shall Babylon, the mighty city, be cast down, and shall be found no more at all.

Even heaven calls our attention to the violence, the suddenness, and the complete annihilation of Babylon. Like a stone that makes a big splash and then disappears beneath the waves will Babylon come to an end.

> And the voice of harpers, and musicians, and of pipers,
> and trumpeters, shall be heard no more at all in thee;
> and no craftsman, of whatsoever craft he be, shall be
> found any more in thee; and the sound of a millstone
> shall be heard no more at all in thee;
>
> And the light of a candle shall shine no more at all in
> thee; and the voice of the bridegroom and of the bride
> shall be heard no more at all in thee: for thy merchants
> were the great men of the earth; for by the sorceries were
> all nations deceived [Rev. 18:22–23].

Again, using my translation: "And the voice of harpers and minstrels
and flute-players and trumpeters shall be heard no more at all in thee."
You see, rock music will go out of style then—and I thank God for
that!

"And no craftsman, of whatsoever craft shall be found any more at
all in thee." All the factories will close down.

"And the light of a lamp shall shine no more at all in thee." All the
neon lights on Broadway will go out.

"And the voice of the bridegroom and the bride shall be heard no
more at all in thee." It's all over—no more marrying and giving in
marriage here.

"For thy merchants were the princes of the earth; for with thy sorcery were all the nations deceived." I believe that more and more we
are going to see sorcery, magic, and demonism. Satanism will increase more and more as we draw neàr the end of the age. It will be
Satan who is going to deceive and blind people, just as he blinds
many in our day.

Popular music comes to an end in Babylon. Jazz and rock 'n' roll
cease in the destruction. Classical music will be stilled, also.

The crafts that have been prostituted to the service of the Antichrist will end. The wheels of the factories will never turn again. The
bright lights of the cities will go out forever. It is interesting to note the
beginning of all these things is recorded in Genesis 4:16–22. Also,
social life and family life shall end. The great tycoons of big business

will disappear. This city deceived the world with the worship of Antichrist—this is the strong delusion.

And in her was found the blood of prophets, and of saints, and of all that were slain upon the earth [Rev. 18:24].

God's people got rough treatment in this city and God judged it. This is Satan's city, and he was a murderer from the beginning. Babylon was a city that murdered; its final crime was the slaying of God's people.

As we contemplate the destruction of Babylon, we think of other great cities and civilizations of the past which have fallen. One of the most widely read books of all time is *The Decline and Fall of the Roman Empire* written by Edward Gibbon in 1788. In it he gives five basic reasons why that great civilization withered and died:

1. The undermining of the dignity and sanctity of the home, which is the basis for human society.

2. Higher and higher taxes; the spending of public money for free bread and circuses for the populace.

3. The mad craze for pleasure; sports becoming every year more exciting, more brutal, more immoral.

4. The building of great armaments when the real enemy was within—the decay of individual responsibility.

5. The decay of religion; faith fading into mere form, losing touch with life, losing power to guide the people.

The oft-heard warning that history repeats itself has an ominous meaning in the light of the above. We can already see these five things at work in our contemporary culture in this country. The same things will bring Babylon down at the end. They destroy the nation and the home and the individual.

Thank God, the sad story of man's sin will come to an end.

This chapter brings to a conclusion the frightful period which was labeled by the Lord Jesus Christ the Great Tribulation. In the next chapter we will see Him coming to the earth to bring to an end this dark, doleful, and disastrous period.

This is the negative aspect to His coming. The positive side is the dawning of the Day of the Lord, called the Millennium or thousand years in chapter 20.

Now let's take a final look at the Great Tribulation period with its catastrophic and cataclysmic events taking place in rapid succession like a machine gun firing.

The total period is seven years. It is the "seventieth week" of Daniel's prophecy. In the Old Testament Daniel divided it, and in the New Testament John divided it into two separate and equal periods of three and one-half years each.

However, after the church leaves this earth, the Antichrist comes to power as world dictator on a platform of peace, prosperity, and fame. During the first part of the Tribulation he will bring about radical changes that seem to benefit mankind. He will bring in a false peace. All government and religion are to be controlled by him. When that time comes, there will be one world, one religion, and one everything. The world will believe that they are entering the Millennium and that the world will become a Utopia. This is part of the big lie of that period. The true church, the body of Christ, will be removed from the earth before the Tribulation begins. It will become the bride of Christ, and we will see this bride shortly—near the end of this book.

Israel will once again become God's witness on earth—144,000 strong, sealed by the Spirit of God. And they will witness here upon the earth. Also, there will be a great company of Gentiles that will be sealed.

Somewhere near the middle of the seven-year period the king of the north, and I believe it will be Russia, will move against Israel. God will judge Russia just as He judged Sodom and Gomorrah. If you want to see that picture, you will find it in Ezekiel 38. This opens the floodgates of war. The Antichrist now begins to move, and the deception, I think, will become apparent to a great many folk. Restless mankind, under the control of Satan, begins to march. The world begins to fall apart, like a pear that is too ripe. The Man of Sin, the Antichrist, breaks his covenant with the nation Israel.

The Mideast will become the center of world activity during this period. Babylon will be the political and economic capital of the world, and Jerusalem (also called Babylon) will be the religious capital. The Antichrist will begin in Rome, and the False Prophet will begin in Jerusalem. Antichrist, when he comes to power, will rebuild Babylon. The apostate church will be destroyed by Antichrist and by the kings of the earth who will be subservient to him.

Ancient Babylon on the Euphrates River will become the political and economic center of the world. If a small nation in the Mideast can turn off the spigot to stop the flow of oil and thereby bring the world to its knees, what will it be when ancient Babylon in that very area becomes again the world center?

New York City will then be a whistle stop on the Toonerville Trolley or not even worth the legendary string of glass beads. Los Angeles will return to an adobe village and no longer will be the city of angels but a dwelling place of demons—it appears as if they are already beginning to move in. London and other great cities of the world will become mere villages with muddy streets. Judgments from God will fall swiftly and suddenly on a God-rejecting and blaspheming world. At one fell swoop one-fourth of the population of the world will be destroyed, and at another time one-third will be blotted out. Nature will be afflicted—the grass and trees of the earth, the sun, moon, and stars in the heavens. One disaster after another will fall on the earth, but the heart of man will still be unrepentant. In fact, he will defy and blaspheme the God of heaven.

Then armies will march toward Israel. For three and one-half years the war will rage. It is not the *Battle* of Armageddon but the *War* of Armageddon. Millions of men will march at that time in that land. They will be engaged in a conflict there, but they will be destroyed. There will be blood up to the bridles of the horses—about four feet deep! That is no exaggeration.

Into this horrible arena of chaos—the chaos of man's making and of Satan's scheming—comes the King of Kings and the Lord of Lords. Yes, the King is coming to the earth but, before all of this can take place, His church must be removed from the earth and go to be with Him. Then the church will return to the earth with Him when He comes to establish His Kingdom. The church is not looking for the fulfillment of any of these things which we have looked at from chapter 4 through chapter 18. The church is looking for the blessed hope and the glorious appearing of our great God and Savior, Jesus Christ.

We do not know the day when Christ will return. We do not even know the period in which He will return. It may be soon. It could be today. On the other hand, He may not return for a hundred years or even several hundred years. No one can say with certainty when the Lord will return for His church. Anyone who sets a date for the Lord's appearing is entirely out of order. Anyone who claims to know when the Lord will return has information that is not in the Word of God.

The best that can be said today is that everything that is happening is significant. We live in a great period in the history of the world, but all we can say for sure is that our salvation is nearer than when we first believed.

The late Dr. Bill Anderson of Dallas, Texas, used to say, "God is getting the stage all set. It looks like He is coming soon. But if He is not planning to come now, and since it would take a lot of doing to get the world in this position again, if I were the Lord, I would just come on now and take the church out of the world."

Well, we hope He will come now, but all we know is that the terrors of the Tribulation will take place after the church has been removed at the Rapture. We have been given no signs by which to gauge the time of His return, but we do see the setting of the stage. And we see some very significant things happening in our day. Obviously, Western Europe is looking for a man strong enough to put the Roman Empire back together. And Antichrist is coming. They may not know it, but they are waiting for him. Also, we see a great power in the north—Russia. Egypt is alive again. China was a sleeping giant that we woke up, and from that great population center they are going to come marching out one of these days. Then the crowning scene of the setting of the stage is Israel, which is back in her land. Everything is in position, the church could be raptured at any moment, and the Tribulation could begin. But it may not. We do not know the day or the hour.

CHAPTER 19

THEME: Marriage of the Lamb and return of Christ in judgment

Now we come to the thrilling events that concern us. In chapter 19 we turn the page to that which marks a drastic change in the tone of Revelation. The destruction of Babylon, the capital of the Beast's kingdom, marked the end of the Great Tribulation. The somber gives way to the song. The transfer is from darkness to light, from the inky blackness of night to a white light, from dreary days of judgment to bright days of blessing. This chapter makes a definite bifurcation in the Book of Revelation and ushers in the greatest event for this earth— the second coming of Christ to the earth to establish His Kingdom. It is the bridge between the Great Tribulation and the millennial Kingdom that He will establish upon this earth. Great and significant events are recorded here. The two central features are the marriage supper of the Lamb and the return of Christ to the earth. One follows the other.

The hallelujahs open this chapter and the opening of hell concludes it. Two great suppers are recorded in this chapter: the marriage supper of the Lamb and the cannibalistic feast of carrion after the last part of the War of Armageddon.

FOUR HALLELUJAHS

As chapter 19 opens, the voices of heaven become one chorus.

And after these things I heard a great voice of much people in heaven, saying, Alleluia; Salvation, and glory, and honour, and power, unto the Lord our God [Rev. 19:1].

As usual, I will give my translation of the literal Greek text throughout this chapter.

> After these things I heard as it were a great voice of a
> great multitude in heaven, saying, Hallelujah; Salva-
> tion, and glory, and honour, and power, unto the Lord our
> God.

"After these things" (Gr.: meta tauta) is an expression we first bumped into when John gave the division of the Book of Revelation in chapter 1, verse 19—literally, "the things that shall be after these things." After what things? After the church things. Chapter 4 opened with meta tauta, and we have been meta tautaing ever since. There is a chronological progression, a sequence of events. Now we will see what will take place after the Great Tribulation. It is recorded in this chapter: the coming of Christ to the earth. He is the only One who can end the Tribulation. And so this is the last occurrence of the expression meta tauta.

"A great voice of a great multitude." In the worship scenes of chapters 5—7 we saw the elders, the church, and the uncounted numbers of angels and created intelligences all worshiping God. Now a great number of tribulation saints has been added to the chorus, and they are going to sing. This is something quite marvelous. This is the first time they have been able to utter the great note of praise of the Old Testament—Hallelujah! This word occurs four times in the first six verses. This is its only occurrence in the New Testament. It is reserved for the final victory. It is interesting to note that hallelujah occurs frequently in the Book of Psalms. It means "praise the Lord." It appears in frequent succession in Psalms 146—150. In fact, Psalm 150 is a mighty crescendo of praise. Hallelujah is a fitting note of praise at this juncture in the Book of Revelation. The Great Tribulation is over. Jesus is coming. The church is to be united with Christ in marriage. Hallelujah! Let's sing it, my friend! Every year I love to hear Handel's Messiah being sung, but regardless of what choir sings it, they don't even touch the rim of the great Hallelujah of this future day. Psalm 104:35 puts it this way: "Let the sinners be consumed out of the earth, and let the wicked be no more. Bless thou the LORD, O my soul. Praise . . . the LORD"—that is, Hallelujah! Hallelujah because God is coming to judge, and the wicked are going to be removed from the earth. Hallelujah is an expletive of praise as the final phase of salvation is coming to pass. This is something that Paul talked about in Romans 8:18–23: "For I reckon that the sufferings of this present time are not worthy to be compared with the glory which shall be revealed in us. For the earnest expectation of the creature waiteth for the manifestation of the sons of God. For the creature was made subject to vanity, not willingly, but by reason of him who hath subjected the same in hope, because the creature itself also shall be delivered from the bondage of corruption into the glorious liberty of the children of God. For we know that the whole creation groaneth and travaileth in pain together until now. And not only they, but ourselves also, which have the firstfruits of the Spirit, even we ourselves groan within ourselves, waiting for the adoption, to wit, the redemption of our body."

My friend, this is that great day which is coming. The earth will be released from the bondage of sin. In the meantime it groans. Go down to the seashore and listen to the waves. One summer I slept by the Atlantic Ocean in a place at Virginia Beach. Every night I was put to sleep by the breaking of the waves on the shore. But the waves were sobbing, as it were, sobbing out their sorrow. Go up in the mountains and listen at night to the wind going through the pine trees. There is not a soprano in all of those pine trees, nor is there a redwood that can sing soprano. Their sounds are all subdued, quiet groans as they await the coming of that great day upon the earth.

And *we* groan. I don't know about you, but I groan. When I was a young man and built my home in Southern California, I used to come bounding down the stairs. Now when I come down the stairs, I groan with every step. My wife says, "You ought not to groan." I tell her that groaning is scriptural. We groan within these bodies, as the Scripture says. I'm all for groaning while we are here. But one day the groaning will be changed to hallelujahs, and that is what John is talking about here.

For true and righteous are his judgments: for he hath judged the great whore, which did corrupt the earth with her fornication, and hath avenged the blood of his servants at her hand.

And again they said, Alleluia. And her smoke rose up for ever and ever.

And the four and twenty elders and the four beasts fell down and worshipped God that sat on the throne, saying, Amen; Alleluia [Rev. 19:2–4].

For true and righteous are his judgments; for he hath judged the great harlot who (formerly) corrupted the earth with her fornication, and he hath avenged the blood of his servants at her hand. And the second time they said, Hallelujah. And her smoke goeth up for ever and ever. And the four and twenty elders and the four living creatures fell down and worshiped God that sitteth on the throne, saying, Amen; Hallelujah.

It is interesting to note that at the conclusion of all these judgments, those in heaven, who have more perfect knowledge than you and I have, are able to say that God's judgments are true and right. If you don't think what God is doing is right, it is because you, not God, are wrong. Your thinking is incomplete, of course, as mine is. God will be righteous in judging the great harlot. This is interesting because when we read about the judgment of the great harlot, representing the apostate church which went into the Tribulation, it says that the kings of the earth and the Antichrist destroyed the harlot. Yet here we are told that it was God who judged it. You see, God uses different instruments, and He will even use the Devil to accomplish His purpose. Those in heaven are saying, "True and righteous are his judgments," because the apostate church deserved to be destroyed; it had made martyrs of many of God's children.

In these verses we find a picture of the church in heaven saying, "Hallelujah." They say it twice. Why? As long as the imposter of the true church, the great harlot, is on the earth, the marriage of the Lamb will not take place in heaven. The anti-church is disposed of first, which makes way for the marriage of the Lamb. I assume that the marriage of the Lamb takes place in heaven sometime during the midst of the Tribulation which is going on upon the earth.

"He hath avenged the blood of his servants at her hand." You see, believers are forbidden to avenge themselves. It is true that some of us try to do it, but the moment we do so, we forsake the walk of faith. In Romans 12:19 God says to us: "Dearly beloved, avenge not yourselves, but rather give place unto wrath: for it is written, Vengeance is mine; I will repay, saith the Lord." God will take care of vengeance for you. If we have been injured, and many of us have been, we want to hit back. That is natural; it is the old nature striking out. However, we are to turn that department over to God. He doesn't intend to let anyone get away with wrong. Vengeance is His. And He will bring judgment on this apostate system.

The twenty-four elders for the first time sing *Hallelujah*. The elders we believe to be the church (see Rev. 4). This is the last time the elders appear as such, for the figure changes now, and the church is to become the bride of Christ. The word *church* means "called out." Here on the earth we are the church, the called-out ones, but after we leave the earth we are the bride.

> **And a voice came out of the throne, saying, Praise our God, all ye his servants, and ye that fear him, both small and great.**
>
> **And I heard as it were the voice of a great multitude, and as the voice of many waters, and as the voice of mighty thunderings, saying, Alleluia: for the Lord God omnipotent reigneth [Rev. 19:5–6].**
>
> *And a voice came forth from the throne, saying, Give praise to our God, all ye his servants, ye that fear him, the small and the great. And I heard as it were the voice of a great multitude, and as it were the voice of many waters, and as it were the voice of mighty thunders, saying, Hallelujah; for the Lord our God, the Almighty reigneth.*

"A voice came out of the throne, saying, Praise our God." Notice that the call to praise comes directly from the throne of God, because the

Lord Jesus Christ is preparing to take control of this world. This is truly the Hallelujah Chorus and the most profound paean of praise in the entire Word of God. It takes us all the way back to that covenant which God made with David in which He promised that He would raise One upon David's throne who would rule the world. In 2 Samuel 7:16 we read: "And thine house and thy kingdom shall be established for ever before thee: thy throne shall be established for ever."

But before Christ returns to the earth, there is going to be a wedding, and you and I, as believers, will be part of it.

BRIDE OF THE LAMB AND MARRIAGE SUPPER

Let us be glad and rejoice, and give honour to him: for the marriage of the Lamb is come, and his wife hath made herself ready.

And to her was granted that she should be arrayed in fine linen, clean and white: for the fine linen is the righteousness of saints [Rev. 19:7-8].

Let us rejoice and be exceeding glad, and let us give the glory unto him; for the marriage of the Lamb is come, and his wife hath made herself ready. And it was given unto her that she should array herself in fine linen, bright and pure; for the fine linen is the righteous acts of the saints.

This will be the most thrilling experience that believers will ever have. The church—that is, the body of believers all the way from Pentecost to the Rapture—will be presented now to Christ as a bride for a marriage. The marriage takes place in heaven, and this is a heavenly scene throughout.

In Ephesians 5 the apostle Paul speaks about the husband and wife relationship when both are believers. By the way, he is speaking of those who are filled with the Spirit and of the relationships that flow from it. You cannot have a Christian home without a Spirit-filled husband and a Spirit-filled wife. In fact, I do not believe you can know what real love is until both marriage partners are believers. Notice Paul's instructions: "Husbands, love your wives, even as Christ also loved the church, and gave himself for it; that he might sanctify and cleanse it with the washing of water by the word, that he might present it to himself a glorious church, not having spot, or wrinkle, or any such thing; but that it should be holy and without blemish" (Eph 5:25–27). This is the picture of the relationship of Christ and the church.

We are living in a day of "new" morality. Our contemporary society is drenched with sex. This generation knows a great deal about sex. I watched a young couple in Palm Springs one day, and I felt sorry for the boy and the girl. They were necking like nobody's business, right in public. I thought to myself, *What do they really know about love? Why, they know nothing about what it means for a man to love a woman and a woman to love a man.* I am afraid there are many Christians who don't know much about love either. Husbands, do you remember the first time you looked at your wife? Do you remember when you were joined in marriage and she became yours? Wasn't that a thrilling moment for you? Wives, do you remember when you first looked at that ugly old boy you married and thought he was so handsome? When he put his arms around you, wasn't that a thrilling moment? Well, Ephesians 5:25–27 is a picture of that day when Christ is going to draw us to Himself, cleansed and purified. Young lady and young man, that is the reason in this day of "new" morality that you should bring purity to your marriage. God have mercy on some of you fellows who are married to second-hand girls. Don't get them at the second-hand store; get them brand new. It is much better that way.

"The marriage of the Lamb is come." Marriage is a marvelous picture of the joining together of Christ and the church. Notice that the Old Testament saints are not included—only the believers during the church age are included. Even John the Baptist designated himself as only a friend of the Bridegroom. He said, "He that hath the bride is the bridegroom . . ." (John 3:29). The bride occupies a unique relationship with Christ. You see, Christ loved the church and gave Himself for it. Remember what He said in His High Priestly Prayer: "I in them, and thou in me, that they may be made perfect in one; and that the world may know that thou hast sent me, and hast loved them, as thou hast loved me. Father, I will that they also, whom thou hast given me, be with me where I am; that they may behold my glory, which thou hast given me: for thou lovedst me before the foundation of the world. O righteous Father, the world hath not known thee: but I have known thee, and these have known that thou hast sent me. And I have declared unto them thy name, and will declare it: that the love wherewith thou hast loved me may be in them, and I in them" (John 17:23–26).

The thing that is so wonderful is that we are going to *know* Christ—really know Him—for the first time.

"The fine linen is the righteous acts of the saints." The wedding gown of the church is the righteous *acts* of the saints. This is a difficult concept to accept, because it is impossible for us to stand before Christ in our own righteousness. Paul wrote of this: "And be found in him, not having mine own righteousness, which is of the law, but that which is through the faith of Christ, the righteousness which is of God by faith" (Phil. 3:9). You see, by faith we can trust Christ—not only for the forgiveness of sins but for the impartation to us of His own righteousness. Then why does John say that the wedding garment is the righteous *acts* of the saints? Well, the wedding gown will be used only once, but we will be clothed in the righteousness of Christ throughout eternity. We as believers will appear before the judgment seat of Christ, not to be judged for our sins in reference to salvation, but for rewards. Through the ages believers have been performing righteous acts which have been accumulating to adorn the wedding gown. By the way, what are *you* doing to adorn that wedding gown? What are you doing for the Lord today?

Again let me quote Paul: "Now if any man build upon this foundation [which is Christ] gold, silver, precious stones, wood, hay, stubble; every man's work shall be made manifest: for the day shall declare it, because it shall be revealed by fire; and the fire shall try every man's work of what sort it is. If any man's work abide which he hath built thereupon, he shall receive a reward" (1 Cor. 3:12–14). Gold, silver, and precious stones will survive the fire; wood, hay, and stubble will go up in smoke. Therefore the good works are the wedding garment of the church. "For we are his workmanship, created in Christ Jesus unto good works, which God hath before ordained that we should walk in them" (Eph. 2:10).

After the wedding, the wedding dress is laid aside. We have already seen that the elders placed their crowns at the feet of the Lamb, proclaiming that He alone is worthy. The church will reveal His glory: "That in the ages to come he might shew the exceeding riches of his grace in his kindness toward us through Christ Jesus" (Eph. 2:7). We will be on display—sinners saved from hell, if you please, in heaven now. We have no right to heaven and would not go there except for the righteousness of Christ and the fact that we belong to Him. The relationship of Christ and the church is intimate, it is different, and it is delightful. No other creatures will enjoy such sweetness.

> **And he saith unto me, Write, Blessed are they which are called unto the marriage supper of the Lamb. And he saith unto me, These are the true sayings of God.**
>
> **And I fell at his feet to worship him. And he said unto me, See thou do it not: I am thy fellow-servant, and of thy brethren that have the testimony of Jesus: worship God: for the testimony of Jesus is the spirit of prophecy [Rev. 19:9–10].**
>
> *And he saith unto me, Write, Blessed are they that are bidden (invited) to the marriage supper of the Lamb. And he saith unto me, These are the true words of God. And I fell down before his feet to worship him. And he saith unto me, See thou do it not; I am a fellow servant with thee and with thy brethren that hold the testimony of Jesus; worship God; for the testimony of Jesus is the spirit of prophecy.*

Hear me carefully now: the marriage of the Lamb will take place in heaven, but the marriage supper will take place upon the earth. The picture of this is in Matthew 25:1–13, which is the parable of the ten virgins. You see, the virgins were not the bride. Christ has only one bride, and that is the church. The Bridegroom will return to the earth for the marriage supper. He will return not only to judge the earth but to have the marriage supper, which the ten virgins are expecting to attend.

Another picture of this same scene is given in Psalm 45. In this psalm Christ is seen coming as king. We are not told who she is, but the queen is there: "Kings' daughters were among thy honourable women: upon thy right hand did stand the queen in gold of Ophir" (Ps. 45:9). I believe this is a symbol or a type of the church.

Guests are present: "And the daughter of Tyre shall be there with a gift; even the rich among the people shall entreat thy favour" (Ps. 45:12). The marriage supper will take place on earth. Both Israelites and Gentiles who enter the Millennium are the invited guests. The marriage supper is evidently the Millennium. You talk about a long supper—*this* is going to be a long one! At the end of the Millennium the church is still seen as the *bride*. Imagine a honeymoon which lasts one thousand years! Yet that is only the beginning. What joy! What ecstasy! The angel puts God's seal on this scene: "These are the true words of God."

After acting as a scribe for this scene, John feels compelled to worship the angelic messenger. However, he is restrained from doing so. The angel is but a creature. Only God is to be worshiped. What a rebuke to Satan, the Antichrist, and the False Prophet who wanted to be worshiped. And there are many folk in our day who have that same desire.

After the marriage of the Lamb in heaven, the next great event is the return of Christ to the earth. My friend, the King is coming! But He will not come until after the church has been raptured and after the earth has undergone the Great Tribulation. Now when He comes to the earth, His bride will be with Him, and their marriage supper will be here upon the earth, as we have seen. Oh, my friend, what a glorious day is ahead of us! If we could only get our eyes off the muck and mire of this earth and onto that which is eternal!

RETURN OF CHRIST AS KING OF KINGS AND LORD OF LORDS

And I saw heaven opened, and behold a white horse; and he that sat upon him was called Faithful and True, and in righteousness he doth judge and make war.

His eyes were as a flame of fire, and on his head were many crowns; and he had a name written, that no man knew, but he himself [Rev. 19:11–12].

And I saw the heaven opened, and behold, a white horse, and he that sat on him was called Faithful and True, and in righteousness doth he judge and make war. Now his eyes a flame of fire, and upon his head many diadems; having a name written which none knew but himself.

What a thrilling scene this is! Just to read it makes goose pimples come out all over me. This is the great climactic event toward which all things in this world are moving today. It is the coming of Christ to the earth.

Let me take a moment to remind you where this fits into the picture. From chapters 4—18 we were in the midst of the Great Tribulation period, a frightful period. It ends by the coming of Christ to this earth to establish His Kingdom.

In the past there has been a very naïve notion relative to the future, which is still held by some folk who are not students of the Bible. It is this: One of these days Jesus is going to come, and all the dead will be raised. The good guys will be on one side and the bad guys on the other. Christ will make the division so that one will enter heaven, the other hell, and eternity begins. May I say again that this is a very naïve notion.

You cannot read the Word of God without being conscious of the fact that He has a plan and program for this earth and that He is following it very carefully. The program, as we have outlined it, reveals

that Christ's return to the earth takes place at the end of the Great
Tribulation period, right before the establishment of His Kingdom.

The contrast to His first coming is stupendous. It is absolutely remarkable.

At the time of Christ's first coming, as George Macdonald put it:

> They all were looking for a King
> To slay their foes and lift them high;
> Thou cam'st, a little baby thing
> That made a woman cry.

That is the way He entered the world the first time. He was meek and
lowly. He was the Savior who died for sinners. Now in the verses before us we see Him coming in His great glory. His coming will be the
final manifestation of the wrath of God upon a sinful world. The rebellion of Satan, demons, and men is contained, put down, and judged.
He puts down all unrighteousness before He establishes His Kingdom
in righteousness.

Heaven is opened in chapter 4, verse 1, to let John, as a representative of the church, enter heaven where he sees the elders, that is, the
church, already there. And here in chapter 19 heaven opens to let
Christ exit. The white horse on which He rides is the animal of warfare. When Jesus was on earth, He rode into Jerusalem upon a little
donkey which, though an animal of kings, denoted peace, not war.

He is called "Faithful" because He has come to execute the long-
time program of God. Remember that the scoffer said, "Where is the
sign of His coming?" There is no sign at this point—He is here. He has
made good. He is Faithful. He is the *only* One you and I can trust and
rest upon.

He is called "True" for He is inherently true. He is not one who just
tells the truth, although He does that; He is the bureau of standards of
truth. He is the yardstick of truth. He *is* the Truth. How wonderful it is
to have Someone in whom to trust in this day when everything we
hear is slanted and used as propaganda.

He has come to "judge and make war"—not to die on a cross again.

"Now his eyes a flame of fire." Back in chapter 1, verse 14, His eyes were *as* a flame, as He walked among the churches, judging them. But now there is a difference—"his eyes a flame of fire" because He has come to judge the earth and put down its unrighteousness.

"Upon his head many diadems" indicates that He will be the sole ruler of this earth. And His rulership is going to be a dictatorship, I can assure you of that. My friend, if you don't love Jesus Christ—if He is not your Savior—and you live to enter this period of His return to the earth, it is going to be a most uncomfortable period for you because Christ is going to be a dictator. A chicken won't peep, a rooster won't crow, and a man will not move without His permission. He is the King of Kings and He is the Lord of Lords.

"And he had a name written, that no man knew." What is this name that no one knew but Himself? He is given four names here which correspond to the Gospels:

1. "King of kings" corresponds to the Gospel of Matthew, since Matthew presents Christ as the King.

2. "Faithful and True" corresponds to the Gospel of Mark where He is presented as the Servant of God. The important thing about a servant is not his genealogy but his trustworthiness. Is he faithful and truthful? Those are the qualities that are important.

3. "Word of God" repeats what He is called in the Gospel of John: "In the beginning was the Word. . . . And the Word was made flesh . . ." (John 1:1, 14).

4. What is the name that no one knows? Well, I have a suggestion. Perhaps it corresponds to Luke's Gospel in which He is presented as Jesus, the Son of Man. In our day there is a great familiarity with that name, both in swearing and in blaspheming and in being overly free and presumptuous with Him. But, my friend, that is a name which you and I are going to probe throughout eternity. He is Jesus, the Son of Man. Do you really know Jesus? Well, no man knoweth the Son but the Father, and here we learn that when He comes, He has a name that no man really knows but Himself.

The apostle Paul, not at the beginning but at the end of his ministry, before his execution, said, "That I may know *him*, and the power of his resurrection, and the fellowship of his sufferings, being made conformable unto his death" (Phil. 3:10, italics mine). No one knows the Son but the Father. My friend, learning to know Him is one of the things that is going to make heaven *heaven*. He is so wonderful that it is going to take the rest of eternity to really know Him. The folk we meet down here are not very exciting folk when we get to know them, are they? But the more we know Jesus, the more exciting He will be.

In John 14:7, 9, we read: "If ye had known me, ye should have known my Father also: and from henceforth ye know him, and have seen him [that is, in the Person of the Son]. . . . Jesus saith unto him, Have I been so long time with you, and yet hast thou not known me, Philip? he that hath seen me hath seen the Father; and how sayest thou then, Shew us the Father?"

Then again in that High Priestly Prayer that Christ prayed: "And this is life eternal, that they might know thee the only true God, and Jesus Christ, whom thou hast sent" (John 17:3). When we come to Christ and receive Him as our Savior from sin, we have started to school. When we begin to know Him, we are in kindergarten. Let me make more or less of a confession. Since I have retired from the pastorate, I have set before me a goal: I want to know Jesus better than I do now. I get up every morning and look out the window—I did *this* morning and in Southern California it is foggy—but I say, "Lord, thank You for bringing me to another day. I love You. I love You, Lord Jesus, but, oh, You seem to be so far away at times. I want to know You. May the Spirit of God make You real to me." The name Jesus—oh, what it means, and what a person He is!

One more thing I would like to say about this subject: not only will we come to know the Lord better throughout eternity, we are also going to get to know one another better. I really don't think we know each other as we should. I find, at times, that I am greatly misunderstood. I make certain statements on the radio, and then I receive letters that almost shock me. It is difficult to understand how I could have been that misunderstood. But in heaven we are going to know as we are known. I think that will be good. Also, we will know ourselves. And we are going to know our loved ones. One summer when I tried to recuperate from an illness by resting, it enabled me to sit on my patio with my wife and get acquainted with her. It was quite wonderful. I discovered the sacrifices that she has made and her faithfulness down through the years. And I think I am *really* going to get acquainted with her in heaven. My friend, how glorious heaven is going to be! Even in this earthly life down here we find that when we grow in our love for Christ, we also grow in our love for each other.

Now notice the further description of Christ at His coming:

> **And he was clothed with a vesture dipped in blood: and his name is called The Word of God.**
>
> **And the armies which were in heaven followed him upon white horses, clothed in fine linen, white and clean.**
>
> **And out of his mouth goeth a sharp sword, that with it he should smite the nations: and he shall rule them with a rod of iron: and he treadeth the winepress of the fierceness and wrath of Almighty God.**
>
> **And he hath on his vestures and on his thigh a name written, KING OF KINGS, AND LORD OF LORDS [Rev. 19:13–16].**

> *And he is arrayed in a garment sprinkled with blood: and his name is called the Word of God. And the armies which are in heaven followed him upon white horses, clothed in fine linen, white and pure. And out of his mouth proceedeth a sharp sword, that with it he should smite the nations; and he shall rule them with a rod of iron: and he treadeth the winepress of the fierceness of the wrath of God the All-ruler. And he hath on his garment and on his thigh a name written, KING OF KINGS, AND LORD OF LORDS.*

Notice that His garment is sprinkled with blood and that He is treading the winepress of the fierceness and wrath of God. This picture takes us back to Isaiah 63:1–6, which we have quoted previously.

Obviously, this refers not to Christ's first coming but to His second coming as described here in chapter 19.

"And he shall rule them with a rod of iron" takes us back to Psalm 2: "Yet have I set my king upon my holy hill of Zion. I will declare the decree: the LORD hath said unto me, Thou art my Son; this day have I begotten thee [from the dead]. Ask of me, and I shall give thee the heathen for thine inheritance, and the uttermost parts of the earth for thy possession. [He didn't get them at His first coming; how will He get them now?] Thou shalt break them with a rod of iron; thou shalt dash them in pieces like a potter's vessel" (Ps. 2:6–9).

The fury of His wrath at His second coming is in sharp contrast to His gentleness at His first coming. However, in both is revealed the "wrath of the Lamb."

"The armies . . . in heaven" are evidently the legions of angels that do His bidding.

THE WAR OF ARMAGEDDON

Now we come to the end of the War of Armageddon, and this concludes the final battle:

> **And I saw an angel standing in the sun; and he cried with a loud voice, saying to all the fowls that fly in the midst of heaven, Come and gather yourselves together unto the supper of the great God;**
>
> **That ye may eat the flesh of kings, and the flesh of captains, and the flesh of mighty men, and the flesh of horses, and of them that sit on them, and the flesh of all men, both free and bond, both small and great [Rev. 19:17–18].**

If there is one passage of Scripture which is revolting to read, this is it. You will notice that God included it at the end of His Word to remind us how revolting and nauseating to Him are the deeds of the flesh. Men who live in the flesh will have their flesh destroyed. This is an invitation at the end of the Battle of Armageddon to the carrion-eating fowl to a banquet on earth where they will have A-1, blue-ribbon flesh

to eat—kings and the mighty men of the earth. My friend, it is frightful to rebel against God because He is going to judge you someday.
This scene reveals the heart of man and how dreadful that heart really
is.

HELL OPENED

Now for the very first time hell is completely opened up:

> **And I saw the beast, and the kings of the earth, and
> their armies, gathered together to make war against
> him that sat on the horse, and against his army.**
>
> **And the beast was taken, and with him the false prophet
> that wrought miracles before him, with which he de-
> ceived them that had received the mark of the beast, and
> them that worshipped his image. These both were cast
> alive into a lake of fire burning with brimstone.**
>
> **And the remnant were slain with the sword of him that
> sat upon the horse, which sword proceeded out of his
> mouth: and all the fowls were filled with their flesh
> [Rev. 19:19–21].**
>
> *And I saw the beast, and the kings of the earth, and their
> armies gathered together to make war against him that
> sat upon the horse and against his army. And the beast
> (Antichrist) was taken, and with him the false prophet
> that wrought the signs in his sight, wherewith he de-
> ceived them that had received the mark of the beast and
> them that worshiped his image: they two were cast alive
> into the lake of fire that burneth with brimstone; and the
> rest were killed with the sword of him that sat upon the
> horse, even the sword which came forth out of his mouth;
> and all the birds were filled with their flesh.*

What a frightful picture this is. The Beast and the False Prophet defy
God right up to the very last. They dare to make war with the Son of

God! Surely "He that sitteth in the heavens shall laugh" at the utter
futility of their efforts. It is preposterous that there is such a rebellion
of man against God. The outcome is inevitable. The two arch-rebels
and tyrants, the Antichrist and the False Prophet, have the question-
able distinction of being the first two who are cast into hell. Even the
Devil hasn't been put there yet.

The question arises: Is the "lake of fire" literal? Well, let me give
you something to think about because I am going to come back to this
subject when we get to chapter 20. If hell is not literal, it depicts that
which is *worse* than a literal fire of brimstone.

"The sword which came forth out of his mouth." What is that
sword? An amillennial friend of mine asked me laughingly, "You
don't believe that there is going to be a literal sword coming out of the
mouth of Jesus, do you?" I told him that I would consider it to be
literal if the Word of God had not made it clear that His Word is like a
sword: "For the word of God is quick, and powerful, and sharper than
any two-edged sword, piercing even to the dividing asunder of soul
and spirit, and of the joints and marrow, and is a discerner of the
thoughts and intents of the heart" (Heb. 4:12). "And take the helmet
of salvation, and the sword of the Spirit, which is the word of God"
(Eph. 6:17). "But with righteousness shall he judge the poor, and re-
prove with equity for the meek of the earth: and he shall smite the
earth with the rod of his mouth, and with the breath of his lips shall
he slay the wicked" (Isa. 11:4). Do you notice how clearly this symbol
is explained by Scripture? The "sword" that comes from the mouth of
Jesus is His Word. It was His Word that created this universe. It is the
Word of God which will save you. And it will be the Word of God that
will destroy the wicked at the end of the age.

CHAPTER 20

THEME: The Millennium

In the twentieth chapter we are dealing with the Millennium in relationship to Christ, Satan, man, the tribulation saints, the resurrections, the earth, and the Great White Throne. Unfortunately, a great many men in the past have thought that chapter 20 is not very important because the Millennium, the thousand-year period, is mentioned only here in Scripture, and therefore, they have practically dismissed this chapter altogether. It is true that the Millennium is mentioned only in this chapter, and it is mentioned as "a thousand years." Let's not argue about semantics. *Millennium* comes from the Latin word that means "one thousand." Millennium means a thousand years any way you slice it. You can call a person who believes in the Millennium a chiliast, and chiliasm is the way the early church spoke of it, because in the Greek *chiliasm* means "a thousand" also. I hope we understand that millennialism, chiliasm, and the thousand-year reign of Christ all refer to the same thing.

Chapter 20 is the division point for the three main schools of eschatology:

Postmillennialism assumed that Christ would come at the conclusion of the one thousand years. Man would bring in the Kingdom by the preaching of the gospel. This was an optimistic view which prevailed at the turn of the century. At that time it looked like there might be a great worldwide turning to Christ and the world would be converted. This viewpoint has become obsolete as it could not weather the first half of the twentieth century, which produced two world wars, a global depression, the rise of communism, and the atom bomb with which worldwide destruction is imminent.

Amillennialism has become popular only in recent years and has largely supplanted postmillennialism. The addition of the prefix *a-* simply negates the belief in the Millennium. Amillennialism holds out no false optimism and has, for the most part, emphasized the coming of Christ. Its chief weakness is that it spiritualizes the thousand years, as it does all the Book of Revelation. It fits the Millennium into the present age. Dr. B. B. Warfield's interpretation is that the Millennium is going on in heaven while the Tribulation is going on down here on the earth. My belief is that in heaven they have a millennium, not just for a thousand years, but from eternity to eternity. Most amillennialists fit the Millennium into the present age, and all the events recorded in Revelation are somehow fitted into the facts of history like pieces are fitted into a crazy quilt. Frankly, I think that the results of this viewpoint are about the same: you come up with a crazy quilt.

Premillennialism, on the contrary, takes chapter 20 at face value, as it does all of the Book of Revelation, applying the literalist interpretation unless the context instructs otherwise. Let me cite the example we gave from chapter 19 where it says that, when the Lord Jesus comes, out of His mouth goes a sharp two-edged sword (see Rev. 19:15). Does this mean that a literal sword goes out of His mouth? I believe that Scripture makes it very clear that the sword is the Word of God. Paul writes, "And take . . . the sword of the Spirit, which is the word of God" (Eph. 6:17). With that kind of instruction, I do not see how we can misunderstand what John is talking about, but you must have a scriptural reason for your interpretation. You cannot spiritualize Scripture on any basis you choose, although that is the present custom and the popular method today. In the premillennialist interpretation, the one thousand years are treated as one thousand years, and Christ comes at the beginning of the Millennium. Chapter 20 makes it clear that there can be no Millennium until Christ comes.

In the first nine verses of this chapter, we have the word for a thousand years repeated six times. It must be pretty important to put that kind of emphasis on it. The early church believed in what was known as chiliasm, the belief in the literal thousand-year reign of Christ. Those who rejected that position were considered to be in a state of heresy. Later on there came in the teaching that the thousand years would be established by the church. The church would produce a perfect world, and then Jesus would come and find everything in apple-pie order. But that is not the way this section of Scripture presents it. He is coming in judgment, and if everything were in apple-pie order, there would be no need to put down rebellion and to judge and make war.

It has not been too long ago that men actually believed that the church was going to build the Kingdom down here on this earth. Back in 1883 a commentator, Justin A. Smith, made this statement:

But upon the other hand, what a tremendous force is the Christianity of today when all is said. Is it conceivable that this auspicious power, which is so rapidly taking possession of the wide earth, can dwindle into the imbecility which some millennarians appear to predict for it?

Those of us who are premillennialists would be called a bunch of pessimists back in 1883 because we are predicting that the world is going to get worse and that there will be apostasy in the church. This man did not believe that, for he goes on to say:

It has been said that in twenty-five years more, if the present rate of progress continues, India will become as thoroughly Christian as Great Britain is today. There will be thirty millions of Christians in China, and Japan will be as fully Christianized as America is now. The old systems, they tell us, are honeycombed through and through by Christian influence. It looks as if a day may soon come when these systems, struck by vigorous blows, will fall in a tremendous collapse. Meantime, every weapon formed against Christianity breaks in the hand that holds it. Already, the Lord's right hand hath gotten Him victory.

But look at Great Britain today, for example—it is as bad off as India is. They talked bravely in those days, but they do not talk that way today. In the book *The Problems of Evil*, the author made this statement:

The civilization of Europe, or to call it by its true name which derives from its origin, the Christian civilization, is visibly making the conquest of the world. Its triumph is only a matter of time. No one doubts it.

There are quite a few who doubt it today. In fact, the so-called European civilization, or Christian civilization, is going down the drink and has largely disappeared already.

These men belittle the twentieth chapter of Revelation. I consider Dr. B. B. Warfield to be the greatest scholar that this century has produced, and I was educated under his system, but he says that there is no reference to such an age as a millennium here on this earth "save in so obscure a portion as Revelation 20." He pays no attention to all of the Old Testament where God made a covenant that He would establish this Kingdom on the earth through One in David's line.

Dr. Rothe many years ago said:

> Our key does not open. The right key is lost. Until we are put in possession of it again, our exposition will never succeed. The system of biblical ideas is not that of our school at all.

In speaking with a student who had read a premillennial book and was enthusiastically telling him about it, Dr. R. L. Dabney, an honored theologian of the South in the past, said, "Probably you are right. I never looked into the subject." He was a great scholar but was honestly admitting that he had never studied prophecy!

The late Dr. Charles Hodge, who wrote two ponderous tomes on theology (and that was the theology I studied when I was in school), very frankly said that eschatology wasn't his bag—only he didn't use that expression:

> The subject cannot be adequately discussed without taking a survey of all the prophetic teaching of the Scriptures, both of the Old Testament and the New. This task cannot be satisfactorily accomplished by anyone who has not made the study of the prophecies a specialty. The author, knowing that he has no such qualifications for the work, proposes to confine himself in a great measure to a historical survey of the different schemes of interpreting the scriptural prophecies relating to the subject.

Today all that has changed. There is a lively interest in prophecy, but I wish there were more who were as honest as Dr. Hodge was and would say, "I really haven't studied the subject as I should have." Unfortunately, a great many men are speaking on the subject of prophecy who have not actually studied it. This is a very important and vital subject. I do not claim to have any specal qualifications for it at all, although I have studied it for forty years and have given a great deal of attention to it, even in the years past when it was largely ignored. But I think it is dangerous today that many are edging up to this matter of setting dates for the rapture of the church. I believe that the Rapture is absolutely a dateless event. It *may* be tomorrow, but it may *not* be tomorrow. We need to recognize that we are living in a period in which we are not given dates, but we are seeing the setting of a stage. I do not know what God has in mind for the future, but I do know that He sure has things in position.

I think it is obvious that I am premillennial and also pretribulational, and the reason is that I believe this is what John is teaching here. If you disagree with me and accept one of these other positions, you are in good company. Some of the finest men I have known hold a different viewpoint from mine, but if you want to be right, you will want to go along with me, of course!

First of all, there can be no Millennium until Satan is removed from the earthly scene. You could not have an ideal state down here as long as Satan is running loose.

In the second place, the curse of sin must be removed from the physical earth before a Millennium can be established. Scripture prophesies that the desert will blossom like a rose. If you live along the coast in California, the desert blossoms like a rose, but in eastern California, the desert is not blossoming like a rose. The curse of sin has not yet been removed from this earth.

In the third place, the resurrection of the Old Testament saints must take place at the beginning of the thousand years. If they were raised before the Great Tribulation, they would have to stand around and wait for the Millennium. There is no need for them to do that, and the Lord is not going to raise them until the Tribulation is over. Daniel makes this very clear: "And at that time shall Michael stand up, the great prince which standeth for the children of thy people: and there shall be a time of trouble, such as never was since there was a nation even to that same time: and at that time thy people shall be delivered, every one that shall be found written in the book. And many of them that sleep in the dust of the earth shall awake, some to everlasting life, and some to shame and everlasting contempt" (Dan. 12:1-2). This is talking about Israel. Following the Great Tribulation period will be the resurrection of the Old Testament saints (see Isa. 25:8-9). Only Christ will raise the dead (see John 5:21, 25, 28-29), so He must come for that purpose.

In the fourth place, the Tribulation saints are included in the resurrection of the Old Testament saints, and they reign with Christ during the Millennium.

Finally, the Millennium is the final testing of man under ideal conditions. This is the answer to those who say there is nothing wrong in man which circumstances and conditions cannot change. Man is an incurable, an incorrigible sinner. Even at the end of the Millennium, he is still in rebellion against God. The rebellion in the human heart and the depraved nature of man are impossible for any man to comprehend. If you and I could see ourselves as God sees us, we could not stand ourselves. But we think we are pretty good and that we are very nice people—do we not? The Millennium is the final testing of mankind before the beginning of the eternal state.

The Millennium is God's answer to the prayer, "Thy kingdom come." When we pray the prayer which we mistakenly call the Lord's Prayer, we say, "Thy kingdom come . . . in earth, as it is in heaven" (Matt. 6:10). That is the Kingdom which He is going to establish here on earth, and it is called the Millennium. This is the Kingdom which was promised to David (see 2 Sam. 7:12-17; 23:5). God took an oath relative to its establishment (see Ps. 89:34-37). This is the Kingdom predicted in the psalms and in the prophets (see Ps. 2; 45; 110; Isa. 2:1-5; 11:1-9; 60; 61:3-62; 66; Jer. 23:3-8; 32:37-44; Ezek. 40—48; Dan. 2:44-45; 7:13-14; 12:2-3; Mic. 4:1-8; Zech. 12:10—14:21). All of the prophets spoke of this Kingdom, the minor prophets as well as the major prophets—not one of them missed it. These are but a few of the manifold Scriptures that speak of the theocratic kingdom which was the great theme of all the prophets in the Old Testament. This is the Kingdom, the theocratic Kingdom, that is coming here upon this earth.

SATAN BOUND ONE THOUSAND YEARS

The opening verses of chapter 20 describe what is to precede the Millennium.

And I saw an angel come down from heaven, having the key of the bottomless pit and a great chain in his hand.

And he laid hold on the dragon, that old serpent, which is the Devil, and Satan, and bound him a thousand years,

And cast him into the bottomless pit, and shut him up, and set a seal upon him, that he should deceive the nations no more, till the thousand years should be fulfilled: and after that he must be loosed a little season [Rev. 20:1–3].

Let me give you my translation of these verses:

And I saw an angel coming down out of the heaven, having the key of the abyss and a great chain in his hand. And he laid hold on the dragon, the old serpent who is the Devil and Satan, and bound him for a thousand years, and cast him into the abyss, and locked and sealed (it) over, that he should deceive the nations no longer, until the thousand years should be finished: after that he must be loosed for a little time.

You will notice that the thousand years are mentioned two times in verses 1–3; they are mentioned a total of six times in the twentieth chapter. It is true that the Millennium is mentioned only in one chapter, but God mentions it six times. How many times does He have to say a thing before it becomes true? He mentions it more than He mentions some other things that people emphasize and think are important just because they occur once or twice in Scripture. Six times the thousand years are mentioned, and here it is in relationship to Satan.

There are some expositors who separate this section from the Millennium, classifying it as the closing scene of the Day of Wrath. This view takes the edge from the sharp distinction that there will be on earth at the removal of Satan. His incarceration and total absence from the earth change conditions from darkness to light. He is the god of this age; he is the prince of the power of the air, and his power and influence in the world are enormous—beyond the calculations of any computer. His withdrawal makes way for the Millennium, for with him loose, there can be no Millennium. Therefore, we see that Satan's relationship to the Millennium is this: he must be removed from the earth's scene before it can take place. Men talk about bringing peace on this earth, about producing prosperity, and all that sort of thing. The world system will finally be headed up in the Antichrist, and he will not be able to accomplish peace and prosperity, although for a while it will look as if he will. But as long as Satan is abroad in this world, you cannot have a Utopia down here. You cannot have an ideal situation with him loose.

"An angel. . . . laid hold on the dragon"—Satan's great power is reduced, for an ordinary angel becomes his jailor and leads him away captive (see Jude 9; Rev. 12:7–9).

"The abyss" is a better description of the prison than is "the bottomless pit." In either case, it is not the lake of fire, which we shall see in verse 10.

"After that he must be loosed for a little time" is one of the imponderable statements of Scripture. Why is Satan loosed after God once had him put in the abyss in chains? Dr. Lewis Sperry Chafer's answer to this question is significant: "If you will tell me why God let him loose in the first place, I'll tell you why God let him loose in the second place." Why did God let him loose? God has a great purpose in it. This is the great problem of evil: Why has God permitted it? Well, I believe that God is working out a tremendous program which is the mystery of God that is yet to be revealed to us. It is going to be revealed someday, and all He is asking us to do is to walk with Him by faith. We need to trust God and know that whatever He is doing is right.

I remember one time when my dad took me with him on a trip in his horse and buggy. A storm came up out there in west Texas and, being just a boy, I was frightened. The wind was blowing up a real storm, and we were getting wet. I never shall forget that my dad put his arm around me and said, "Son, you can trust me." I just snuggled right up to him and trusted him, and we got through the storm. My earthly father is gone—he died when I was fourteen. I didn't have my earthly father very long, but I have had a heavenly Father now for a great many years whom I trust through the storms of this life. In all these problems that come up, I wish I had the answers to give you, but I don't—so let's both trust Him.

I once read a book on the problem of evil. When I finished the book, we still had the problem of evil—the author did not solve it. It took him about two hundred pages to say what I can say in one sentence: I do not know the answer to the problem of evil. But, my friend, we will get the answer someday if we walk by faith.

God had Satan incarcerated for one thousand years because there could not be a Millennium without that.

SAINTS OF THE GREAT TRIBULATION REIGN
WITH CHRIST ONE THOUSAND YEARS

And I saw thrones, and they sat upon them, and judgment was given unto them: and I saw the souls of them that were beheaded for the witness of Jesus, and for the word of God, and which had not worshipped the beast, neither his image, neither had received his mark upon their foreheads, or in their hands; and they lived and reigned with Christ a thousand years.

But the rest of the dead lived not again until the thousand years were finished. This is the first resurrection.

Blessed and holy is he that hath part in the first resurrection: on such the second death hath no power, but

they shall be priests of God and of Christ, and shall reign with him a thousand years [Rev. 20:4–6].

And I saw thrones and they sat upon them, and judgment was given unto them; and (I saw) the souls of them that had been beheaded for the testimony of Jesus, and for the Word of God; and whosoever worshiped not the wild beast neither his image, and received not the mark upon their forehead, or upon their hand. And they lived again and reigned with Christ one thousand years. This is the first resurrection. Blessed and holy is he that hath part in the first resurrection; over these the second death hath no authority [Gr.: exousian], but they shall be priests of God and of the Christ, and shall reign with him a thousand years.

Many are going to die for Christ in the Great Tribulation period, but they will live again and reign with Christ one thousand years. The Tribulation saints are going to trade in three and one-half years for one thousand years. I would say they are getting a pretty good deal. Those three and one-half years will be rugged and terrible, but the thousand years are going to be wonderful—imagine living and reigning with Christ upon this earth!

This prophecy is like any other prophecy in Scripture: "Knowing this first, that no prophecy of the scripture is of any private interpretation" (2 Pet. 1:20). That is, you cannot just lift out a verse of Scripture and base doctrine on it; you need to have the corroboration of other Scriptures. When this passage here is treated as a dignified statement of literal facts, it becomes reasonable, and it fits into the entire program of prophecy which we have been following. Any attempt to reduce it to the lowest common denominator of fanciful and figurative symbols makes the passage an absurdity. To spiritualize this passage is to disembowel all Scripture of vital meaning, making the interpretation of Scripture a *reductio ad absurdum.*

The thrones are literal; the martyrs are literal; Jesus is literal; the Word of God is literal; the Beast is literal; the image is literal; the mark of the Beast is literal; their foreheads and their hands are literal; and the thousand years are literal. It is all literal. A thousand years means a thousand years. If God meant that it was eternal, I think He would have said so. If He meant it was five hundred years, He would have said so. Cannot God say what He means? Of course He can, and when He says a thousand years, He means a thousand years.

The Greek word for "resurrection" is *anastasei*, which means "to stand up, a bodily resurrection." It is rather difficult for a spirit to stand up, and those who spiritualize this section are at a loss to explain just how a spirit stands up! This is the same word used by Paul in 1 Corinthians 15 for the resurrection of Christ and believers.

"And I saw thrones and they sat upon them" is the one statement that is not entirely clear. Who are "they"? It is my judgment that they must be the total number of those who have part in the first resurrection, which includes the saved of all ages.

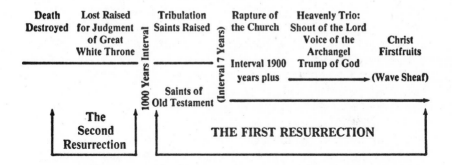

The first resurrection began with the resurrection of Christ. Then it is followed by the resurrection (at the Rapture) of His church sometime more than nineteen hundred years later—but before the Great Tribulation (see Rev. 4). At the end of the Great Tribulation is the resurrection of both the Tribulation saints ("the souls of them that had been beheaded for the testimony of Jesus, and for the Word of God; and whosoever worshiped not the wild beast") and the Old Testament saints (see Dan. 12:1–2). The diagram above gives the resurrection as a parade. Christ, the firstfruits of resurrection, leads the parade.

It is a rather simple and naïve notion to think that somehow or another the world is going to end, Jesus will come, the dead will be raised, He will put the good guys on one side and the bad guys on the other, they will move into eternity, and that is it. My friend, God follows a very definite program; He always has, and He moves intelligently.

The Tribulation saints and the Old Testament saints will evidently reign on this earth with Christ. I believe that David will be His vicegerent. The church, which is the bride of Christ, will reside in the New Jerusalem where she reigns with Him from that exalted place and, I believe, over a great deal of God's creation. Christ will commute from the New Jerusalem to the old Jerusalem on this earth. And I suppose that the church also will travel back and forth between its heavenly home and the earth.

Multitudes of both Israel and the Gentiles will enter the Kingdom in natural bodies, not having died. These are the ones, together with those who are born during the Millennium, who are tested during this millennial period. As Christ in a glorified body mingled with His apostles and followers, so the church in glorified bodies will mingle with the multitudes in their natural bodies here on the earth. In glorified bodies, the church will be able to move out into space. That will be the first time I will do any space traveling. I can assure you of that. Gravitation will not be able to grab me by my pants and pull me back to the earth in that day.

"They shall be priests of God" refers to the entire nation of Israel. This was God's original purpose for Israel: "And ye shall be unto me a kingdom of priests, and an holy nation. These are the words which thou shalt speak unto the children of Israel" (Exod. 19:6). Abraham was a priest in his family. Levi was the priestly tribe, with the family of Aaron serving as high priest. In the theocratic kingdom here on this earth, the entire nation of Israel will be priests.

In Scripture there is more prophecy concerning the Millennium than of any other period. The Kingdom was the theme of the Old Testament prophets. I do not know how else you would interpret it. In our day we hear very little about the minor prophets. There is a great silence, a great vacuum and void, when it comes to the teaching of the minor prophets, yet all of them look forward to the Millennium, that Kingdom which is coming on the earth.

SATAN LOOSED AFTER ONE THOUSAND YEARS

And when the thousand years are expired, Satan shall be loosed out of his prison,

And shall go out to deceive the nations which are in the four quarters of the earth, Gog and Magog, to gather them together to battle: the number of whom is as the sand of the sea.

And they went up on the breadth of the earth, and compassed the camp of the saints about, and the beloved city: and fire came down from God out of heaven, and devoured them [Rev. 20:7–9].

And when the thousand years are ended Satan shall be loosed out of his prison, and shall come forth to deceive the nations which are in the four corners (quarters) of the earth, Gog and Magog, to gather them together to the war; the number of whom is as the sand of the sea. And they went up over the breadth of the earth, and compassed the camp of the saints about, and the beloved city: and fire came down out of heaven, and devoured them.

Although the entire Book of Revelation deals with last things, especially do these last few chapters. Here is the last rebellion of Satan and man against God. The Millennium is a time of testing of man under ideal conditions, as this passage demonstrates. As soon as Satan is released, a great company, who have been under the personal reign of Christ under ideal circumstances, goes over to Satan. From where did such a company come is a worthy question. The answer lies in the fact that not only do multitudes enter the Millennium, but multitudes also are born during the Millennium (see Isa. 11:6; 65:20). This will be the time of the earth's greatest population explosion. Disease will be eliminated. Since the curse of sin will be removed from the physical earth, it will produce enough foodstuffs to feed its greatest population. The human heart alone remains unchanged under these circumstances, and many will turn their backs on God and will go after Satan. This seems unbelievable, but what about today? Satan is doing pretty well in our day.

This rebellion following the Millennium reveals how terrible the heart of man is. Jeremiah said, "The heart is deceitful above all things, and desperately wicked: who can know it?" (Jer. 17:9). You and I do not know how vile we really are. We just cannot bring our old nature into subjection to God. "Because the carnal mind is enmity against God: for it is not subject to the law of God, neither indeed can be" (Rom. 8:7). These folk will live under ideal conditions during Christ's thousand-year reign, and I think they will get a little tired of it. When He reigns, He is really going to be a dictator—you had better stay in line or else. But they do not like staying in line; therefore, when the opportunity is offered to them to rebel, they rebel. The nations of the earth again will come under the spell of Satan and will plot a rebellion.

Because the rebellion is labeled "Gog and Magog," many Bible students identify it with the Gog and Magog of Ezekiel 38—39. This is not possible at all, for the conflicts described are not parallel as to time, place, or participants—only the names are the same. The invasion from the north by Gog and Magog in Ezekiel 38—39 breaks the false peace of the Antichrist and causes him to show his hand in the midst of the Great Tribulation. That rebellion of the godless forces from the north will have made such an impression on mankind that after one thousand years, that last rebellion of man bears the same label—Gog and Magog.

We have passed through a similar situation in this century. World War I was so devastating that when war again broke out in Europe, involving many of the same nations and even more, it was also labeled a World War, but it was differentiated by the number two. We have World War I, World War II, and people today are predicting World War III.

I can use a further illustration from my personal life. In my family there were so many Johns on both sides of the family that my mother decided I should be J. Vernon McGee. My "J" stands for John, but I have never been called John. An uncle, two grandfathers, and my dad were all named John. So you will understand why I bear the name of J. Vernon—I had to be separated from that crowd. Just because we had a similarity of names does not mean that we were all the same person.

The war in Ezekiel 38—39 relates to Gog and Magog I, and the reference here in Revelation 20:8 is to Gog and Magog II. Although the names are the same, this is a different war, the last rebellion of Satan. Just because the two events involve the same names does not mean they are the same.

In verse 9 there is the dropping of the last "atomic bomb." The phrase, "from God," is actually not in the best texts. It simply means that natural forces which destroyed Gog and Magog I will destroy Gog and Magog II.

This last resistance and rebellion against God was as foolish and futile as man's first rebellion in the Garden of Eden. Here it is not the beginning but the ending of man's disobedience to God. It is the finality of man's rebellion. Nothing remains now but the final judgment.

SATAN CAST INTO THE LAKE OF FIRE
AND BRIMSTONE

And the devil that deceived them was cast into the lake of fire and brimstone, where the beast and the false prophet are, and shall be tormented day and night for ever and ever [Rev. 20:10].

And the devil that deceived them was cast into the lake of fire and brimstone, where are also the wild beast and the false prophet; and they shall be tormented day and night for ever and ever.

This is a most solemn statement, and it is rejected by this lovey-dovey age in which we live. However, it is a relief to God's child to know that the enemy—both his and God's—will at last be brought to permanent justice. There is nothing here to satisfy the curiosity or the sadistic taste. The fact is stated in a reverent reticence which is awe-inspiring. If man had written this, having said this much, he could not have restrained himself from saying more. In that Sir Robert Anderson calls "the wild utterances of prophecy mongers," we see that men do not hesitate to go farther than does the Word of God. The Word of God is very restrained—very little is said about this subject of hell, or even of heaven.

There are several facts here that contradict popular notions. First of all, the Devil is not in hell today. He is the prince of the power of the air. He is the one who controls this world to a large extent. God has limited him in our day, of course, but in the Great Tribulation period, he will have full rein for a while.

In the second place, the Devil is not the first to be cast into hell. The wild Beast and the False Prophet will precede him by one thousand years.

Finally, hell is described as a lake of fire and brimstone. The Lord Jesus is the One who gave the most solemn description of hell. Consider these Scriptures: "Then shall he say also unto them on the left hand, Depart from me, ye cursed, into everlasting fire, prepared for the devil and his angels" (Matt. 25:41). "But the children of the kingdom shall be cast out into outer darkness: there shall be weeping and gnashing of teeth" (Matt. 8:12).

This ought to make anyone stop and think: How can hell be outer darkness and also a literal fire? Jesus Christ also said: "And shall cast them into a furnace of fire: there shall be wailing and gnashing of teeth" (Matt. 13:42). "Where their worm dieth not, and the fire is not quenched" (Mark 9:44). In my thinking, fire is the best symbol that could be used of the reality that hell is. For instance, how are sins that men have committed in the spirit to be punished in the body? I believe that to be in outer darkness and the abyss is to be separated from God and to look back upon a life which has been misspent in this world. Can you think of any fire that would be hotter than for a man in hell to hear the voice of his son saying, "Dad, I followed you down here"? This is a solemn thing. A man asked Dr. Bill Anderson, "Suppose we get over there and find out that what you preach about hell is not true at all?" Dr. Anderson replied, "Then I will just have to apologize and say that I must have misunderstood the Lord. But suppose we get over there and find that it is true? What then?" My friend, it is true; this is the Word of God that we are looking at. We love John 3:16, but what do we think about this?

Fire is a very weak symbol of the reality of what it means to be lost, to be separated from God for eternity. You cannot reduce these descriptions to something less than the reality, because a symbol is always a poor representative of the real thing. Nor can you dissolve this into the thin air of make-believe. The reality far exceeds the description, and human language is beggarly in trying to depict the awful reality. Hell is a place; it is also a state. It is a place of conscious torment. This is the language of the Word of God—you cannot escape it.

SETTING OF GREAT WHITE THRONE
WHERE LOST ARE JUDGED

And I saw a great white throne, and him that sat on it, from whose face the earth and the heaven fled away; and there was found no place for them [Rev. 20:11].

The Great White Throne is what men mistakenly call the general judgment. It is general only in the sense that all the *lost* of all ages are raised to be judged here. All who are saved have been raised in the first resurrection. Even the Tribulation saints had part in the first resurrection. This is the second resurrection in which the lost are raised to be given an equitable, fair, and just evaluation of their works in respect to their salvation.

A man on his deathbed said to me, "Preacher, you just don't need to talk to me about the future. I'll take my chances. I believe God is going to be just and righteous and let me present my works."

I told him, "You are right. He is just and righteous, and He will let you present your works. That is what He says He is going to do. But I have news for you: At that judgment nobody is saved, because you cannot be saved by your works. When you stand in the white light of the righteous presence of God, your little works will seem so puny that they won't amount to anything at all."

The other day our little grandson brought to his grandmother some flowers that he had picked. I want to tell you, they were a sad looking bunch of flowers. With great pride he gave them to his grandmother, and his grandmother patted him on the head and thanked him for the lovely flowers. As I looked at that scene, I could not help but smile, but I also immediately recognized how solemn it is going to be when a lot of these goody-goody boys stand with their little, bitty bouquets in the presence of a Christ whom they have rejected. They expect that He will be like a grandmother who will pat them on the head and say, "What a smart boy you were!" My friend, this is solemn, and this is serious. You need Him as Savior in order to stand in His presence; you need to be clothed with the righteousness of Christ. Don't you know that without this we are sinners and we are *lost?*

We like to compare ourselves with other people: "I'm as good as the Joneses down the street." Sure you are, but you ought to know about the Joneses! It was Samuel Johnson who said, "Every man knows that of himself which he dares not tell his dearest friend." You know yourself, don't you? You know things that you have covered up and smothered that you would not reveal for anything in the world. The Lord Jesus is going to bring them out at this judgment; while you are presenting your little bouquet, He is going to tell you about yourself. My friend, you need a Savior today.

This is the Great White Throne, and the holiness of this throne is revealed in the reaction of heaven and earth to it: "from whose face the earth and the heaven fled away." Of this, John F. Walvoord, in his book *The Revelation of Jesus Christ,* comments:

The most natural interpretation of the fact that earth and heaven flee away is that the present earth and heaven are destroyed and will be replaced by the new heaven and new earth. This is also confirmed by the additional statement in 21:1 where John sees a new heaven and a new earth replacing the first heaven and the first earth which have passed away.

REVELATION 20   157

The One seated on the throne is the Lord Jesus Christ: "For the Father judgeth no man, but hath committed all judgment unto the Son. . . . For as the Father hath life in himself; so hath he given to the Son to have life in himself; and hath given him authority to execute judgment also, because he is the Son of man. Marvel not at this: for the hour is coming, in the which all that are in the graves shall hear his voice, and shall come forth; they that have done good, unto the resurrection of life; and they that have done evil, unto the resurrection of damnation" (John 5:22, 26–29).

What is the work of God? It is to ". . . believe on him whom he hath sent" (John 6:29). Those who have done good are they who have accepted Christ, and they come forth unto the resurrection of life—that is the first resurrection. They who have done evil come forth unto the resurrection of damnation and condemnation—that is the Great White Throne judgment.

And I saw the dead, small and great, stand before God; and the books were opened: and another book was opened, which is the book of life: and the dead were judged out of those things which were written in the books, according to their works.

And the sea gave up the dead which were in it; and death and hell delivered up the dead which were in them: and they were judged every man according to their works [Rev. 20:12–13].

And I saw the dead, great and small, standing before the throne; and books were opened; and another book was opened, which is the book of life; and the dead were judged out of the things which were written in the books, according to their works. And the sea gave up the dead that were in it; and death and Hades gave up the dead that were in them; and they were judged every one according to their works.

Yes, my friend, you will be able to get a fair trial there. Your life is on tape, and Christ happens to have the tape. When He plays it back, you will be able to listen to it, and it is not going to sound good to you, by any means. Are you willing to stand before God and have Him play the tape of your life? I think He will have it on a television screen so that you can watch it, too. Do you think your life can stand the test? I do not know about you, but I could not make it. Thank God for His grace—"For by grace are ye saved through faith; and that not of yourselves: it is the gift of God" (Eph. 2:8).

The dead are classified as the small and the great. They are all lost, for evidently some have their names written in the Book of Life. They had never turned to God for salvation. The Lord Jesus said that in His generation ". . . ye will not come to me, that ye might have life" (John 5:40). These folk standing before His throne had not come.

These are books which record the works of all individuals. God keeps the tapes, and He will play them at the right time. There will be a lot of politicians who will have their tapes played in that day, and there will be a lot of public figures—even preachers—who will have their tapes played in that day, and they are not going to be happy about it. If you are saved, you are going to be happy about it. If you are saved, you are not going to stand before this judgment. Your works are to be judged as a child of God at the judgment seat of Christ, which will be for the purpose of rewards (see 2 Cor. 5:10). The Great White Throne judgment is the judgment of the lost. Multitudes want to be judged according to their works. This is their opportunity. The judgment is just, but no one is saved by works.

"And the sea gave up the dead that were in it." Multitudes who have gone to a watery grave in which the chemicals of their bodies have been dissolved in the waters of the sea will be raised. God will have no problem with this. After all, they are only atoms. He just has to put them together again. He did it once; He can do it again. The graves on earth will give up their bodies; and hades, the place where the spirits of the lost go, will disgorge for this judgment.

And death and hell were cast into the lake of fire. This is the second death.

And whosoever was not found written in the book of life was cast into the lake of fire [Rev. 20:14–15].

And death and Hades were cast into the lake of fire. This is the second death even the lake of fire. And if any were not found written in the book of life, he was cast into the lake of fire.

You will notice that in my translation I have changed "death and hell were cast into the lake of fire" to "death and *Hades* were cast into the lake of fire." *Sheol* or *hades* (translated *hell* in the New Testament) is the place of the unseen dead and is divided into two compartments: paradise and the place of torment (see Luke 16:19–31). Paradise was emptied when Christ took the Old Testament believers with Him at His ascension. "Wherefore he saith, When he ascended up on high, he led captivity captive, and gave gifts unto men. (Now that he ascended, what is it but that he also descended first into the lower parts of the earth? He that descended is the same also that ascended up far above all heavens, that he might fill all things)" (Eph. 4:8–10). Christ did two things: He gave gifts to men down here, but He also took with Him to heaven those Old Testament saints who had died and were in the place called paradise. But the place of torment will deliver up the lost at the judgment at the Great White Throne. All who stand at this judgment are lost, and we are told that they are cast into the lake of fire, which is the second death. The Lord also called it "outer darkness." We believe that this is symbolic of something worse than literal

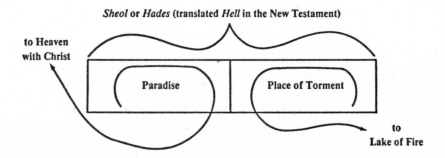

Sheol or *Hades* (translated *Hell* in the New Testament)

to Heaven with Christ

Paradise

Place of Torment

to Lake of Fire

fire or outer darkness. It is eternal separation from God, for death means separation.

"Death," the great final enemy of man, is finally removed from the scene. No longer will it be said, "In Adam all die" (see 1 Cor. 15:22). Death is personified in this case, for it is man's great enemy. In the Old Testament we read: "I will ransom them from the power of the grave; I will redeem them from death: O death, I will be thy plagues; O grave, I will be thy destruction: repentance shall be hid from mine eyes" (Hos. 13:14).

And Paul writes: "The last enemy that shall be destroyed is death. . . . O death, where is thy sting? O grave, where is thy victory?" (1 Cor. 15:26, 55).

"Hades," the prison of lost souls, is likewise cast into the lake of fire. The lost are no longer in hades but in the lake of fire. This is where Satan, the wild Beast, the False Prophet, and their minions were consigned. If man will not accept the life of God, he must accept the only other alternative: eternal association with Satan. God never created man to be put in this place, but there is no other place for him. Hell was created for the Devil and his angels. I take it that it is a place where God never goes. The second death means eternal and absolute separation from God.

CHAPTER 21

THEME: Entrance into eternity; eternity unveiled

Eternity is unveiled in chapter 21—a new heaven, a new earth, a New Jerusalem, a new era, and the eternal abode of the Lamb's bride where we will be new creations in Christ Jesus without the old nature that manifests itself so much today. Adopting a popular aphorism of the day, it can truly be said that this chapter is "out of this world." This chapter hasn't anything to do with the earth (except for the first few verses). In it we see the eternal abode of the church. What really is heaven? There is a lot of sticky, sentimental stuff said about heaven, and we get quite weepy when we talk about heaven. However, heaven is a place, a very definite place. You will have an address there. Your name will be put on you so that in eternity, when you wander around into outer space and get lost, some angel will bring you home—and you will have a home.

As the long vista of eternity is before us in this chapter, we move not only from time to eternity, but to a new creation. A new heaven, a new earth, and a New Jerusalem greet us. The redeemed have previously received glorified bodies like Christ's. All things have become new. A new universe suggests new methods and approaches to life. New laws will regulate the new universe. The entire lifestyle will change. Here are some of the changes that are suggested in chapters 21—22:

1. There will be a total absence of sin and temptation and testing in the new creation. This in itself makes a radical difference.

2. The New Jerusalem, coming down from God out of heaven, does not mean another satellite for the earth, but rather the earth and all of the new creation with all of the galactic systems will revolve about the New Jerusalem, because it is the dwelling place of God and of Christ.

3. The law of gravity, as we know it, will be radically revised. There will be traffic between the New Jerusalem and the earth. The

church will have already left the earth, and its dwelling place is the New Jerusalem. I believe that we will have entirely different bodies, and the law of gravity will not affect us; that is, the law of gravity of this earth or of any other planet.

4. There will be no sun to give light, for God Himself will supply it directly to the universe. There will be the absence, therefore, of night. There is no night there because we just do not need that time to rest since we will have new bodies. I am looking forward to that, by the way.

5. There will no longer be any sea on the earth. The sea occupies most of the earth's surface today; approximately three-fourths of the total surface is water. This denotes a revolution in life upon the earth. Just think of the parking space we will be able to have! There will be no fish to eat. Apparently man will be a vegetarian during the Millennium and throughout eternity, as he was in the Garden of Eden. Fruit is the only diet of eternal man (see Rev. 22:2).

6. The presence of Christ and God, together with the throne of God made visible, ushers in a new day for man—the new creation.

NEW HEAVEN, NEW EARTH, NEW JERUSALEM

John describes the passing of the heaven and earth we know in the opening verse of chapter 21.

> **And I saw a new heaven and a new earth: for the first heaven and the first earth were passed away; and there was no more sea [Rev. 21:1].**

As usual, I'll follow the Authorized Version with my own literal translation of the Greek text.

> *And I saw a new heaven and a new earth: for the first heaven and the first earth passed away: and the sea is no more.*

"And I saw" is the oft repeated statement of John to remind us that he was a spectator to all of these scenes. He was a witness to the panoramic final scene which ushers in eternity.

The Scripture clearly teaches that this present order of creation is to pass away in order to make room for a new heaven and a new earth. The Lord Jesus Christ Himself said, "Heaven and earth shall pass away . . ." (Matt. 24:35). The old creation was made for the first Adam. Christ, the Last Adam, has a new creation for His new creatures. "For, behold, I create new heavens and a new earth: and the former shall not be remembered, nor come into mind" (Isa. 65:17). "For as the new heavens and the new earth, which I will make, shall remain before me, saith the LORD, so shall your seed and your name remain" (Isa. 66:22).

God had promised Abraham a land forever and David a throne forever. Daniel prophesied of ". . . a kingdom, which shall never be destroyed . . ." (Dan. 2:44). The new earth will see the total fulfillment of these prophecies. Consider the faith of the Old Testament worthies: "These all died in faith, not having received the promises, but having seen them afar off, and were persuaded of them, and embraced them, and confessed that they were strangers and pilgrims on the earth. For they that say such things declare plainly that they seek a country. And truly, if they had been mindful of that country from whence they came out, they might have had opportunity to have returned. But now they desire a better country, that is, an heavenly: wherefore God is not ashamed to be called their God: for he hath prepared for them a city" (Heb. 11:13–16). "Heavenly" does not mean they are going to heaven, but that heaven is coming to this earth. This is what we mean when we pray the so-called Lord's Prayer, "Thy kingdom come . . . in earth, as it is in heaven" (Matt. 6:10).

"Nevertheless we, according to his promise, look for new heavens and a new earth, wherein dwelleth righteousness" (2 Pet. 3:13). In his second epistle Peter declares plainly that the present earth on which we live will be destroyed by fire: "But the heavens and the earth, which are now, by the same word are kept in store, reserved unto fire against the day of judgment and perdition of ungodly men. . . . But the day of the Lord will come as a thief in the night; in the which the heavens shall pass away with a great noise, and the elements shall melt with fervent heat, the earth also and the works that are therein shall be burned up. Seeing then that all these things shall be dissolved, what manner of persons ought ye to be in all holy conversation and godliness" (2 Pet. 3:7, 10–11).

The chief characteristic of the new earth, as we have suggested, is the absence of the sea. This would automatically change the climate, the atmosphere, and the lighting conditions. It is impossible for the human mind to comprehend the great transformations which will take place in a new creation. The sea in the past has been a barrier and also a border for mankind, which in some cases has been good and in others bad. Also, the sea was an instrument of judgment at the time of the Flood. However, by the disappearance of the sea, the population on the earth can be doubled again and again because of the increase of the land surface.

And I John saw the holy city, new Jerusalem, coming down from God out of heaven, prepared as a bride adorned for her husband [Rev. 21:2].

And I saw the holy city, new Jerusalem, coming down out of heaven from God, made ready as a bride adorned for her husband.

This is the part which should interest us. I believe that the New Jerusalem is where those of us who are children of God are going to live. When you talk about going to heaven, what do you think about it? To most people it is just "a beautiful isle of somewhere." However, it is a definite place. It is a city called the New Jerusalem. It is a planet within itself. Very candidly, very little is said in Scripture about heaven—but here it is, and that is the reason this ought to be important to us.

"I saw the holy city, new Jerusalem, coming down out of heaven from God, made ready as a bride adorned for her husband." This New Jerusalem should not be identified with the old Jerusalem, the earthly Jerusalem down here.

I cannot think of a lovelier description than this: ". . . made ready as a bride adorned for her husband." It has been my privilege in my many years in the pastorate to have married several hundred couples. I have never seen an ugly bride—they are always lovely. At the wedding ceremony, after the solos have been sung, the preacher walks in followed by the bridegroom and the best man. Nobody pays any attention to the bridegroom except his mama. She smiles at him and thinks he's wonderful, but nobody else looks at him. In a minute here comes the bride-to-be and, I tell you, everybody stands up and looks at her. I have never yet seen an ugly bride. On occasion when I would return from a wedding which my wife did not attend, she would always ask me, "Was the bride beautiful?" And I would always answer, "Yes. I've never seen an ugly one." Don't think that I am just a doting old man when I say that. I have seen some brides *before* they got married or *after* the wedding, and I have wondered if she were the same girl who had come down the aisle. God gives to them at that time a radiance and a beauty. That is a thrilling moment for the bridegroom to look down the aisle and see the one whom he is going to make his own— she will belong to him. It seems that for that moment God transforms every girl into a lovely bride. I think the reason He does it is that the New Jerusalem where we are going to live is like the bride adorned for her husband. What a picture we have here!

The New Jerusalem is the habitation, the eternal home that is prepared for the church. The Lord Jesus said: "I go to prepare a place for you. And if I go and prepare a place for you, I will come again, and receive you unto myself; that where I am, there ye may be also" (John 14:2–3). You could not have a more lovely or more appropriate picture given. We have seen in Revelation 19:7–8 that ushering in the millennial period, actually before Christ returned to the earth, was the marriage of the Lamb, and the bride was the church.

This passage is the fulfillment of what Paul wrote to the Ephesians: "Husbands, love your wives, even as Christ also loved the church, and gave himself for it; that he might sanctify and cleanse it with the washing of water by the word" (Eph. 5:25–26).

At the judgment seat of Christ, there will be the straightening out and the judging of believers. Everything that is wrong will have to be corrected. All sin will be dealt with there. Rewards will be given out. And He is going to do something else—He is going to cleanse the church with the Word. The Word of God is a mighty cleansing agent. "That he might present it to himself a glorious church, not having spot, or wrinkle, or any such thing; but that it should be holy and without blemish" (Eph. 5:27).

This is the picture we are getting here in chapter 21. The holy city, the New Jerusalem, is coming down from God out of heaven, adorned as a bride for her husband. The marriage took place before the Millennium, and the Millennium is now over. This has sure been a long honeymoon, hasn't it? I think it is one that will go on into eternity.

Paul continues to talk about this marvelous relationship between Christ and the church, comparing it to human marriage down here. "So ought men to love their wives as their own bodies. He that loveth his wife loveth himself. For no man ever yet hated his own flesh; but nourisheth and cherisheth it, even as the Lord the church; for we are members of his body, of his flesh, and of his bones. For this cause shall a man leave his father and mother, and shall be joined unto his wife, and they two shall be one flesh. This is a great mystery: but I speak concerning Christ and the church" (Eph. 5:28–32). This idea is a mystery that is now being opened to us. The marriage relationship is the most beautiful and wonderful relationship. It is the oldest ceremony that God has instituted for man. It goes right back into the Garden of Eden, to the very beginning, and it is all-important. It is such a profound mystery that, even with all these marriage counselors and all the books they have written, I do not really think they have touched the fringe of how wonderful marriage *could be* for believers.

By the way, Paul is talking here to believers who are filled with the Spirit. All of these instructions are for Spirit-filled believers. They are not given to the lost world at all, and they are not given to the average believer. At the beginning of this section Paul says, ". . . be filled with the [Holy] Spirit" (Eph. 5:18). That is the only commandment in Scripture in which you are required to do something about the Holy Spirit.

We find here something that is difficult to understand, but it gives us another insight into marriage. The wife is the same flesh as the man. How can that be? Have you ever seen a beautiful child that looked like the mother and had a mean disposition like the father? That is where they come together, that is where they are one flesh. But it is deeper than that. When a man loves his wife, he actually loves himself. This is true of the wife also. When she loves her husband, she is actually loving herself. You cannot have it any more intimate than that.

When I injure my foot, I do not ignore it. I do all I can to care for it. I go to the doctor and if necessary have it put into a cast. It may not be very pretty, and I might like to leave my foot at home, but it is part of me. Likewise, my wife is part of me. She is my flesh. We are the same flesh. This is difficult to understand, but that is how intimate it is. This takes us back to the time of creation: "And Adam said, This is now bone of my bones, and flesh of my flesh: she shall be called Woman, because she was taken out of Man. Therefore shall a man leave his father and his mother, and shall cleave unto his wife: and they shall be one flesh. And they were both naked, the man and his wife, and were not ashamed" (Gen. 2:23–25). They were naked, and they knew each other. It was an *intimate* and a *very personal* relationship. After a couple gets married, when they have their first fight, the wife often turns over in bed, and he is in a huff and maybe goes to the sofa and lies there. Then they wonder why there is disintegration in their marriage relationship. When your foot gets sick, you don't ignore it. You don't get angry with it. You don't kick with it. If you do, you are in deeper trouble. The thing that you are to do with the flesh is to do everything to doctor it and try to get it well again. This is the reason that young couples ought never to have a squabble without sitting down and talking things over. I think the wife ought to be very frank with her husband and tell him everything—how she feels, how he offends her, and what she thinks is wrong. And he ought to do the same thing. You see, they are the same flesh; they are one. They have been brought together in this very intimate, this very wonderful relationship in which a man leaves his family—his father, his mother, and his brothers and sisters. He has now been joined to a woman, and they are one flesh. They have started a new creation, if you please, and that is what the marriage relation should be. How wonderful it is to see a family where the man and his wife have no barrier between them. She knows him like a book, and he knows her like a book. They simply know each other, and they love each other. Until that kind of relationship is established, my friend, you are going to have trouble in the marriage, because God made us that way. Marriage is more than an arrangement to live together and to sleep together. When a man chooses a wife and a wife accepts her husband, they must understand that they are one flesh—and you would not hurt yourself, your own flesh, intentionally for anything in the world.

"This is a great mystery," Paul says, ". . . but I speak concerning Christ and the church" (Eph. 5:32). In heaven we are going to be like Him. John writes, ". . . it doth not yet appear what we shall be: but we know that, when he shall appear, we shall be like him . . ." (1 John 3:2). We are going to have glorified flesh like He has. We are going to be one with Him. We are part of His body, and we are going to be joined to Him. He said, ". . . I go to prepare a place for you: . . . that where I am, there ye may be also" (John 14:2–3). How glorious that we can be with Him throughout eternity! As far as I know, no other creatures, including the angels of heaven, are going to have this personal and intimate relationship with the Lord Jesus Christ. That is going to be the most glorious day! We are going to celebrate throughout eternity the very fact that we are *with* Him and that we have been joined to Him.

NEW ERA

And I heard a great voice out of heaven saying, Behold, the tabernacle of God is with men, and he will dwell with them, and they shall be his people, and God himself shall be with them, and be their God.

And God shall wipe away all tears from their eyes; and there shall be no more death, neither sorrow, nor crying, neither shall there be any more pain: for the former things are passed away [Rev. 21:3–4].

And I heard a great voice out of the throne saying, Behold the tabernacle [Gr.: skene, tent] of God (is) with

*men, and He shall tabernacle with them, and they shall
be His peoples, and God Himself shall be with them,
and be their God; and God shall wipe away every tear
from their eyes; and death shall be no more, neither shall
there be mourning, nor crying nor pain, any more; the
first things are passed away.*

"Behold the tabernacle [tent] of God is with men." What is the tent?
We are told by John in John 1:14, "And the Word was made flesh, and
dwelt [pitched His tent] among us. . . ." That flesh was crucified on the
cross, and He was raised in a glorified body. We, too, are going to have
glorified bodies, and we are going to live with Him in the New Jerusalem. The golden street is not really important. What difference does it
make what kind of asphalt you walk on? It *is* important to know the
psychological and spiritual values that will be there.

"They shall be His people, and God Himself shall be with them,
and be their God." Certain things that definitely are prominent today
are going to be removed: "God shall wipe away every tear from their
eyes." A columnist years ago wrote: "For every light that burns on
Broadway, there is a broken heart." Several times my wife and I have
driven up into the Hollywood hills and have looked down on that
blanket of light which is Hollywood. I have said to my wife, "For
every light down there, there is a broken heart." There is many a sad
and lonely person in this world, but in the New Jerusalem there are
not going to be any more tears.

"And death shall be no more"—that is going to be a very marvelous improvement. Since you began reading this chapter, a number of
funeral processions have taken place. People are dying all the time.
There is a continual march to the cemetery. I once knew an engineer
who in the early days had a great deal to do with the planning and
plotting of the great freeways which crisscross this country today. I
asked him, "Is it going over the mountains or down through the valleys or crossing the rivers that is the biggest problem for you?" He
replied, "The big problem is missing the cemeteries." This earth is a
great cemetery today, but all of that is going to end. There will be no
burying ground in the New Jerusalem. The undertaker will be out of

business. Even the doctors are going to be out of business because there is not going to be any crying, ". . . neither shall there be any more pain: for the former things are passed away."

And he that sat upon the throne said, Behold, I make all things new. And he said unto me, Write: for these words are true and faithful [Rev. 21:5].

And He that sitteth on the throne said, Behold, I make all things new. And He saith, Write, for these words are faithful and true.

He is going to make all things new! This is more meaningful to me than anything else. I do not know about you, but I have never really been satisfied with this life. I have found myself frustrated, I have found myself hemmed in, and I have never been able to accomplish all that I have wanted to accomplish. I've never been the man I've wanted to be. I've never been the husband I've wanted to be. I've never been the father I've wanted to be. And I've never preached the sermon I've wanted to preach. I just do not seem to have arrived. All accomplishments seem to have a blot on them.

But He says to me, as He says to you, "I am going to make all things new. You are going to be able to start over again." I am waiting for that day when all things are going to be new and I can start over. Have you ever stopped to think about the potential of starting out all new again, of learning all over again, and never ceasing but going on into eternity? Oh, the potential and capability of man! Yonder at the Tower of Babel, God said, "I had better go down there, or nothing will be withheld from man" (see Gen. 11:5–7). It was very foolish for some scientists and preachers to say that man could not go to the moon; I think he is going farther than that. Man is a clever being which God has made. Death ends his potential down here, but with eternity ahead of him, oh, the prospects a saved man has!

We see here the glorious prospect of all things made new. We can start over, and there will never be an end to our growth. Remember that of Christ it is said, "Of the increase of His government and peace there shall be no end" (see Isa. 9:7). There is constant growth and development. Just think of the prospect of that for the future. Someday I am going to know something; today I don't, but I will then.

And he said unto me, It is done. I am Alpha and Omega, the beginning and the end. I will give unto him that is athirst of the fountain of the water of life freely.

He that overcometh shall inherit all things; and I will be his God, and he shall be my son [Rev. 21:6–7].

And He said unto me, They are come to pass. I am the Alpha and the Omega, the beginning and the end. I will give unto him that is athirst of the fountain of the water of life freely. He that overcometh shall inherit these things; and I will be God unto him, and he shall be the son to Me.

"I am the Alpha and the Omega, the beginning and the end." This identifies the speaker as the Lord Jesus Christ, as He was identified like this in the first chapter of this book.

Believers in their new bodies will thirst after God and the things of God, and they will be satisfied: "I will give unto him that is athirst of the fountain of the water of life freely." In Matthew 5:6 the Lord Jesus said: "Blessed are they which do hunger and thirst after righteousness: for they shall be filled."

All believers are overcomers because of faith: "He that overcometh shall inherit these things." "For whatsoever is born of God overcometh the world: and this is the victory that overcometh the world, even our faith" (1 John 5:4).

"I will be God unto him, and he shall be the son to Me." All the sons of God become sons through faith in Christ: "But as many as received him, to them gave he power to become the sons of God, even to them that believe on his name" (John 1:12).

They "inherit all things" because this was promised to the sons of God: "The Spirit itself beareth witness with our spirit, that we are the children of God: and if children, then heirs; heirs of God, and joint-heirs with Christ; if so be that we suffer with him, that we may be also glorified together" (Rom. 8:16–17).

"The son to Me" is in the Greek *moi ho huios*. This is a very unusual expression. Vincent calls attention to the fact that this is the only place in John's writings where a believer is said to be a son *(huios)* in relationship with God. (In other passages another Greek word is used rather than *huios*.) God is the One who says "my son," and He says it here. Believers in the church are one of the peoples of God, but they are more. They are the sons of God in a unique and glorious fashion. "Beloved, now are we the sons of God, and it doth not yet appear what we shall be: but we know that, when he shall appear, we shall be like him; for we shall see him as he is" (1 John 3:2).

But the fearful, and unbelieving, and the abominable, and murderers, and whoremongers, and sorcerers, and idolaters, and all liars, shall have their part in the lake which burneth with fire and brimstone: which is the second death [Rev. 21:8].

But for the fearful, and unbelieving, and defiled with abominations, and murderers, and fornicators, and sorcerers, and idolators, and all liars, their part (shall be) in the lake that burneth with fire and brimstone: which is the second death.

There are several amazing features about this verse. First of all, the creation of the new heavens and a new earth did not affect the status of the lake of fire and of the lost. They are going into eternity just that way.

In the second place, there is no possibility of sin, which made man become fearful, unbelieving, liars, murderers, and all the rest, ever breaking over the barriers into the new heavens and the new earth. Sin and its potential are forever shut out of the new creation.

Finally, the lake of fire is eternal, for it is the second death, and there is no third resurrection. It is eternal separation from God, and there is nothing as fearful and frightful as that.

NEW JERUSALEM, DESCRIPTION OF THE
ETERNAL ABODE OF THE BRIDE

The appearance of this city is the quintessence of beauty, refined loveliness, and uncontrolled joy. Lofty language describes her merits, and descriptive vocabulary is exhausted in painting her portrait. The contemplation of her coming glory is a spiritual tonic for those who grow weary on the pilgrim journey down here.

The New Jerusalem is really a postmillennial city, for she does not come into view until the end of the Millennium and the beginning of eternity. This city was evidently in the mind of Christ when He said, "I go to prepare a place for you" (see John 14:2), but the curtain does not rise upon the scene of the heavenly city until earth's drama has reached a satisfactory conclusion. Earth's sorrow is not hushed until the endless ages begin.

The New Jerusalem will be to eternity what the earthly Jerusalem is to the Millennium. The earthly Jerusalem does not pass away, but it takes second place in eternity. Righteousness *reigns* in Jerusalem; it will *dwell* in the New Jerusalem. Imperfection and rebellion exist even in the earthly Jerusalem during the Millennium; perfection and the absence of sin will identify the heavenly city. Just as a king's queen is of more importance than the place of his government, thus the New Jerusalem transcends the city of earth. This will cast no reflection on the earthly city, nor will it cause her inward pain. She can say in the spirit of John the Baptist, "She that hath the bridegroom is the bride" (see John 3:29).

The New Jerusalem is the eternal abode of the church. The New Jerusalem is the home of the church, the hometown of the church. This is a city toward which the church is journeying as she pitches her tent in that direction. We are now to look at this new home by reading the architect's blueprint in this twenty-first chapter.

And there came unto me one of the seven angels which had the seven vials full of the seven last plagues, and talked with me, saying, Come hither, I will shew thee the bride, the Lamb's wife [Rev. 21:9].

> *And there came one of the seven angels who had the*
> *seven bowls, who were laden with the seven last plagues;*
> *and he spoke with me, saying, Come hither, I will show*
> *thee the bride, the wife of the Lamb.*

What follows in verses 9–21 is a description of the city. We have seen
the psychological or spiritual aspects of it that are wonderful, but this
physical description is also worth contemplating.

We must pause here to consider the relationship of the city to the
citizens—the city proper to the church. Certainly we are not to infer
that the empty city without the citizens is the bride. The citizens are
identified with the city in chapter 22, verses 3, 6, 19. Those outside
are identified here in verse 8 as disfranchised. Although a distinction
between the bride and the city needs to be maintained, it is the intent
of the writer to consider them together.

This passage is a description of the adornments which reveal
something of the love and worth that the Bridegroom has conferred
upon His bride.

> **And he carried me away in the spirit to a great and high**
> **mountain, and shewed me that great city, the holy Jeru-**
> **salem, descending out of heaven from God [Rev. 21:10].**
>
> *And he carried me away in the Spirit to a mountain great*
> *and high, and showed me the holy city Jerusalem, com-*
> *ing down out of heaven from God.*

Certainly this city has no counterpart among earth's cities which are
built upon an earthly foundation and are built up from that base. This
city comes down out of heaven. She originates in heaven, and the Lord
Jesus is the builder. Although the city comes down out of heaven,
there is no suggestion that she comes down to the earth. The earthly
city never goes to heaven, and the heavenly city never comes to earth.
Just how far down the city descends is a matter of speculation.

This has led to extreme views in interpreting the New Jerusalem.
At the very beginning, Ebionism, one of the first heresies, went to the

extreme of applying this whole passage concerning the New Jerusalem to the earthly Jerusalem. The Gnostics, another early heresy, went to the other extremity in spiritualizing the passage to make it refer to heaven. Many modern "isms" apply the New Jerusalem to themselves and set it up on earth at the geographical location of their choice. Liberal theologians and amillennarians have left the city in heaven, in spite of the scriptural statement that it comes down "out of heaven." Two facts are evident from this passage: (1) It comes down out of heaven, and (2) it is not stated that it comes to the earth. This passage of Scripture leaves the city hanging in midair. This is the dilemma that many seek to avoid, but why not leave the city in midair? Is anything incongruous about a civilization out yonder in space on a new planet? The New Jerusalem will either become another satellite to the earth or, what is more probable and what I think is true, the earth will become a satellite to the New Jerusalem as well as the rest of the new creation. This chapter indicates that the city will be the center of all things. All activity and glory will revolve about this city. God will be there, it will be His headquarters, and His universe is theocentric (God-centered). The New Jerusalem is therefore worthy to merit such a preeminent position for eternity.

> **Having the glory of God: and her light was like unto a stone most precious, even like a jasper stone, clear as crystal [Rev. 21:11].**

> *Having the glory of God: her light was like unto a stone most precious, as it were a jasper stone, shining like crystal.*

Paul instructs the believers to ". . . rejoice in hope of the glory of God" (Rom. 5:2). This hope will be realized in the holy city. Man in sin has never witnessed the revelation of the glory of God. The experience of Israel in the wilderness taught them that each time there was a rebellion in the camp, the glory of God appeared in judgment. The manifestation of God's glory strikes terror to a sinful heart, but what glorious anticipation to be able to behold His glory when standing clothed in the righteousness of Christ!

Two wonderful facts make this city the manifestation of the fullness of God's glory. (1) The presence of God makes the city the source of glory for the universe. Every blessing radiates from the city. (2) The presence of the saints does not forbid the manifestation of the glory of God. Sin caused God to remove His glory from man's presence, but in this city all that is past. Redeemed man dwelling with God in a city "having the glory of God" is the grand goal which is worthy of God. This city reveals the high purpose of God in the church, which is to bring "many sons unto glory" (see Heb. 2:10).

The word translated "light" (*phoster*) is the Greek word for source of light. The city is a light giver. It does not reflect light as does the moon, nor does it generate light by physical combustion like the sun, but it originates light and is the source of light. The presence of God and Christ gives explanation to this, as He declared, ". . . I am the light of the world" (John 9:5). God is light.

The whole city is like a precious gem. This gem is likened unto a jasper stone. The modern jasper is a multicolored quartz stone. The stone referred to here cannot be that, for this stone is not opaque. "Jasper" is a transliteration of the word *iaspis*, which is of Semitic origin. Moffatt suggests that *iaspis* could mean the modern opal, diamond, or topaz.

The stone is transparent and gleaming, which suggests one of these stones, most likely the diamond. The diamond seems to fit the description better than any other stone known to man. The similarity of the Hebrew word for crystal in Ezekiel 1:22 to the Hebrew word for "ice" helps to strengthen this view. The New Jerusalem is a diamond in a gold mounting. This city is the engagement ring of the bride; in fact, it is the wedding ring. It is the symbol of the betrothal and wedding of the church to Christ.

THE GATES OF THE CITY

And had a wall great and high, and had twelve gates, and at the gates twelve angels, and names written thereon, which are the names of the twelve tribes of the children of Israel:

On the east three gates; on the north three gates; on the south three gates; and on the west three gates [Rev. 21:12–13].

Having a wall great and high; having twelve (large) gates, and at the gates twelve angels; and names written thereon, which are the names of the twelve tribes of the children of Israel: on the east (day spring) were three gates; and on the north three gates; and on the south three gates; and on the west three gates.

There are twelve gates to the city, three gates on each side. On each gate is the name of one of the tribes of Israel. This is very striking and suggests immediately the order in which the children of Israel camped about the tabernacle in the wilderness wanderings. The tribe of Levi was the priesthood and served in the tabernacle proper. The New Jerusalem is a temple or tabernacle in one sense, for God is there dwelling with man. The bride constitutes the priesthood who serve Him constantly. They serve as such in the city and dwell there as Levi did about the tabernacle.

Everything in eternity will face in toward this city, for God is there. The children of Israel on earth will enjoy the same relationship to the city that they did toward the wilderness tabernacle and later the city temple. This city will be a tabernacle to Israel. The children of Israel will be among the multitudes who come into this city to worship in eternity. They will come from the earth to bring their worship and glory. They will not dwell in the city anymore than they dwelt in the tabernacle of old. Those who actually dwell there will be the priests, who are the bride. The bride occupies the closer place to God in eternity, and the bride, like John in the Upper Room, reclines upon His breast. "Who is this that cometh up from the wilderness, leaning upon her beloved? . . ." (Song 8:5). She is the bride, and she has come up from the wilderness which is this present world. But the twelve tribes of Israel will come up to the celestial city to worship, three tribes coming up on each of the four sides. They will then return back to the earth after a period of worship, but the bride will dwell in the New Jerusalem.

THE FOUNDATIONS OF THE CITY

And the wall of the city had twelve foundations, and in them the names of the twelve apostles of the Lamb [Rev. 21:14].

This city has twelve foundations, and the names of the twelve apostles are upon them. The church today is ". . . built upon the foundation of the apostles and prophets, Jesus Christ himself being the chief corner stone" (Eph. 2:20). When Christ returned to heaven, He committed the keys into the keeping of the apostles. On the human level, the church was in the hands of these twelve men. The Book of Acts gives the order: "The former treatise have I made, O Theophilus, of all that Jesus began both to do and teach, until the day in which he was taken up, after that he through the Holy Ghost had given commandments unto the apostles whom he had chosen" (Acts 1:1–2). I do not believe that Matthias is the apostle who succeeded Judas. I personally believe it was Paul. Simon Peter held that meeting to elect Matthias before the Holy Spirit came, and I do not think he was in the will of God when he did so. You never hear Matthias mentioned again, but you surely hear of Paul the apostle, and I think he is the one whom God chose to succeed Judas, making Paul the twelfth apostle.

To these twelve apostles were committed all the writings of the church. These men preached the first sermons, they organized the first churches, and they were among the first martyrs. It is not honoring to Scripture to attempt to minimize the importance of the twelve apostles. In a real sense they were the foundation of the church. To them the church shall eternally be grateful. This is not to rob Christ of His place, for He is "the chief corner stone," but the church is built upon the foundation which the apostles laid.

THE SIZE AND SHAPE OF THE CITY

And he that talked with me had a golden reed to measure the city, and the gates thereof, and the wall thereof.

> And the city lieth foursquare, and the length is as large
> as the breadth: and he measured the city with the reed,
> twelve thousand furlongs. The length and the breadth
> and the height of it are equal [Rev. 21:15–16].

The shape of this city is really difficult to describe, due largely to our inability to translate our concepts from a universe of time to the new creation of eternity. The measurements of the city have given rise to all sorts of conceptions as to the size and shape of the city. First of all, let us examine the size of the city. Twelve thousand furlongs is given as the measurement of each side and the height of it. It is twelve thousand *stadia* in the text, which means about fifteen hundred miles. This figure is corroborated by Dr. Seiss, Dr. Walter Scott, and others. The amplitude of the city is astounding when first considered but is commensurate with the importance of the city. Certainly God as Creator can never be accused of stinting, economizing, or doing things that reveal littleness. When you go down to the beach, you notice that He has put plenty of sand there and plenty of water in the ocean. He has made many mountains and He has put rocks everywhere. With a lavish hand, He has garnished the heavens with stellar bodies. When He does something, He certainly does it in abundance. This city bears the trademark of its Maker. The Lord Jesus, the Carpenter of Nazareth, is the One who built this city.

Now consider with me the shape of the city. ˙ he city lieth foursquare" is the simple declaration of Scripture. That would seem to indicate that the city is a cube with fifteen hundred miles on a side. Dr. Seiss sees it as a cube. Dr. Harry Ironside sees it as a pyramid. Still others interpret these measurements in as many geometric figures as can be conceived. However, it is difficult for us to conceive of either a cube or a pyramid projected out in space. We are accustomed to thinking of a sphere (that is a ball-shaped object) hanging in space, because that is the general shape of the heavenly bodies. As far as we know, there are none out there that are square like a cube or like a pyramid. Cubes and pyramids are appropriate for earth's buildings, but they are as impractical for space as spheres are impractical for earthly buildings. Yet it is definitely stated that the city is foursquare.

The difficulty resolves when we think of the city as a cube within a crystal-clear sphere. What we are given are the *inside* measurements. I think of it as a big plastic ball with a cube inside, having all eight of its corners touching the sphere. As this involves mathematics, which I could not figure out, I asked both a mathematician and an engineer involved in the space program to determine what the circumference of the sphere would be. They both came up with the same answer. To enclose a cube measuring 1,500 miles on each side, the circumference of the sphere would be about 8,164 miles. The diameter of the moon is about 2,160 miles, and that of the New Jerusalem sphere is about 2,600 miles. Thus, the New Jerusalem will be somewhat larger than the moon, and it will be a sphere like the other heavenly bodies. I personally believe that this is the picture that is given to us here.

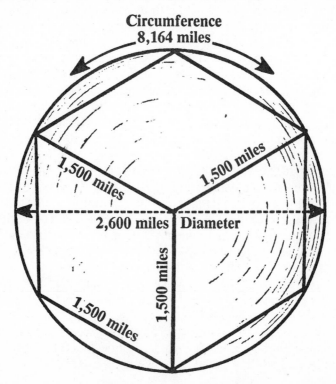

**Circumference
8,164 miles**

1,500 miles

1,500 miles

2,600 miles   Diameter

1,500 miles

1,500 miles

My thinking is that we will live *inside* this sphere, not on the outside. Here on earth, we live on the outside, and that presents a few difficulties. The Lord had to make the law of gravity to hold us on the earth, or we would be flying out into space. We walk on the outside here, but I think that we will walk on the inside of the New Jerusalem.

THE WALL OF THE CITY

And he measured the wall thereof, an hundred and forty and four cubits, according to the measure of a man, that is, of the angel.

And the building of the wall of it was of jasper: and the city was pure gold, like unto clear glass [Rev. 21:17–18].

The wall of the city is for protection. A walled city is a safe city. The New Jerusalem is safe, and those who dwell therein dwell in safety. The heavenly Salem will enjoy the fruits of safety and peace. Made up of those who found peace with God on earth, she will experience the fullness of peace throughout eternity. The walls are a sign that this city has achieved the full meaning of her name—peace.

The walls are 144 cubits in height or about 216 feet. Herodotus gives the estimation for the walls of ancient Babylon as 50 cubits thick and 200 cubits high. Those walls were built to make the city impregnable. The great height of the walls of the New Jerusalem are but commensurate with the great size of the city. Beauty, rather than protection, is the motive in design. It is a wall with jasper built into it and is generally designated as a jasper wall. The hardest of substances and the most beautiful gem constitute the exterior of the city.

THE STONES OF FIRE IN THE FOUNDATION

And the foundations of the wall of the city were garnished with all manner of precious stones. The first foundation was jasper; the second, sapphire; the third, a chalcedony; the fourth, an emerald;

> The fifth, sardonyx; the sixth, sardius; the seventh,
> chrysolyte; the eighth, beryl; the ninth, a topaz; the
> tenth, a chrysoprasus; the eleventh, a jacinth; the
> twelfth, an amethyst [Rev. 21:19-20].

The twelve foundations of the city not only have the names of the
twelve apostles, but they are twelve different precious stones. The
most beautiful and costly articles known to man are precious stones.
These stones express in human terms the magnificence of the city.
The superlative degree of gems is used to convey something of the
glory of the city to those who now ". . . see through a glass, darkly . . ."
(1 Cor. 12:11). We are going to see through it clearly someday.

A close examination of these twelve stones in the foundation reveals a polychromed paragon of beauty; varied hues and tints form a
galaxy of rainbow colors. The stones are enumerated as follows:

1. Jasper (Gr: *iaspis*)—its color is clear. As mentioned before, this
is probably the diamond. It is crystal clear, a reflector of light and
color. Dr. Seiss, in speaking of the New Jerusalem, describes it "as
clean, and pure, and bright as a transparent icicle in the sunshine."

2. Sapphire (Gr.: *sappheiros*)—its color is blue. This stone occurs
in Exodus 24:10 as the foundation of God, ". . . and there was under
his feet as it were a paved work of a sapphire stone, and as it were the
body of heaven in his clearness." Moffatt describes it as a blue stone.
Pliny describes it as opaque with gold specks, to which Petrie agrees.

3. Chalcedony (Gr.: *chalkedon*)—its color is greenish. It is an ag-
ate. Pliny describes it as "a variety of emerald gathered on a mountain
in Chalcedon." Robertson says, "Possibly a green silicate of copper."

4. Emerald (Gr.: *smaragdos*)—its color is green. Robertson describes it as a green stone.

5. Sardonyx (Gr.: *sardonux*)—its color is red. Robertson describes
it as white with layers of red.

6. Sardius (Gr.: *sardios*)—its color is fiery red. Pliny says that it is
the red stone from Sardis. Swete says that it is fiery red.

7. Chrysolyte (Gr.: *chrusolithos*)—its color is golden yellow. Moffatt assigns it a golden hue. Robertson says it is a golden color like our
topaz.

8. Beryl (Gr.: *berullos*)—its color is green. It is like the emerald, says Robertson. Pliny says it is sea green.

9. Topaz (Gr.: *topazion*)—its color is greenish yellow. Robertson calls it a golden greenish stone.

10. Chrysoprasus (Gr.: *chrusoprasos*)—its color is gold-green. A golden leek, "a leek colored gem," says Robertson. The *International Standard Bible Encyclopedia* describes it as sea green.

11. Jacinth (Gr.: *huakinthi*)—its color is violet. It is the color of the hyacinth. Pliny gives the color as violet.

12. Amethyst (Gr.: *amethustos*)—its color is purple. Although the *International Standard Bible Encyclopedia* lists it as a ruby, Robertson gives the color as purple.

The foundations of the New Jerusalem are constructed of the flashing brilliance of rich and costly gems. On the inside is Jesus who, when He was here, was the Light of the World. There He will be the Light of the Universe. Astronauts tell us that in space the colors almost entirely are gray and black—but wait until you see the New Jerusalem. It is going to light up God's new heavens and new earth as they have never been lighted before. I think it is going to be the most breathtaking sight that you have ever seen. This New Jerusalem is a planet which comes down right out of heaven. Everything is going to revolve around it, and the light will come from there. It truly will be the Jesus Christ Light and Power Company then. The light will shine out in all these brilliant and beautiful colors.

Color is described to us today as dissected light. If you pass a ray of light through a prism, it is broken up into three primary colors: red, blue, and yellow. From these three primary colors come all colors and shades of colors. Light is a requirement for color. Where there is no light, there is no color. Objects of color reveal color to the eye because of their ability to absorb or to reject light rays. A red stone absorbs all the color rays except red; it rejects or throws back to the eye the red ray, which gives it the color of red.

The New Jerusalem is a city of light and a city of color. God is light, and He is there. The city is described as a jasper stone as clear as crystal. All of this color will be coming out and flooding God's universe. The jasper stone is a sphere, and the city, the New Jerusalem, is within. The light shining from within through the jasper stone, acting as a prism, would give every color and shade of color in the rainbow—colors that you and I have not even thought of yet. The New Jerusalem is, I believe, a new planet, and it is inside a crystal ball. The presence of the primary colors suggests that every shade and tint is reflected from this city. A rainbow that appears after a summer shower gives only a faint impression of the beauty in the coloring of the city of light. Oh, what a glorious place this is!

THE CITY AND STREET OF GOLD

And the twelve gates were twelve pearls: every several gate was of one pearl: and the street of the city was pure gold, as it were transparent glass [Rev. 21:21].

Notice that verse 18 also says, "and the city was pure gold, like unto clear glass." We were told at the beginning of this description that this city is transparent. This is the thing that gave me the lead and the key to believe that we will live on the inside and that everything is transparent. This would mean that the light shines from the inside out and goes through these many different-colored stones. Many colors which our natural eyes cannot see today we will be able to see with the new body that we shall have at that time.

We are also told here that the street is pure gold. Personally, I do not care about the asphalt of the place, but there are two things here that impress me. (1) It is not streets (plural) but street (singular)—this is not a city with many streets. (2) And it is "transparent"—even the street is transparent; it is gold, but transparent gold.

This leads me again to insist that what we are looking at is the inside of a globe. You could not have cities like we have today without having streets. You would certainly have a traffic jam with just one street. The New Jerusalem has just one street, which would begin at the four gates; it would start around the circle of the globe, go all the way to the top, and then circle and come back down. One would be the entrance and the other the exit. There is just one street, and my viewpoint lends itself to the idea that there is one street. The fact that it is transparent gold means that the light can shine out. There will be nothing to hinder the light, not even the street.

NEW RELATIONSHIP—GOD DWELLING WITH MAN

And I saw no temple therein: for the Lord God Almighty and the Lamb are the temple of it.

And the city had no need of the sun, neither of the moon, to shine in it: for the glory of God did lighten it, and the Lamb is the light thereof [Rev. 21:22–23].

God lights the new creation directly by His presence. After the entrance of sin into the old creation, God withdrew His presence, and "darkness covered the face of the deep" (see Gen. 1:2). Then God made use of the physical lights in His universe. He put them up like we put up street lights or lights in our homes. However, in the new creation sin is removed, and He again becomes the source of light. Today the Lord Jesus Christ is the Light of the World in a spiritual sense: "Then spake Jesus again unto them, saying, I am the light of the world: he that followeth me shall not walk in darkness, but shall have the light of life" (John 8:12).

In the new creation He is the direct physical as well as the spiritual light. In the tabernacle there was the golden lampstand, which is one of the finest pictures of Christ. In the New Jerusalem He *is* the golden lampstand. The nations of the world will enter the Holy City as the priests entered the Holy Place in the tabernacle for the purpose of worship. The nations of the earth, as well as Israel, will come to the New Jerusalem as the high priest of old entered the Holy of Holies. Instead of the blood being brought, the Lamb is there in person. What a picture we have here!

The temple, which supplanted the tabernacle back in the nation Israel, was an earthly enclosure for the *shekinah* glory. It was a testimony to the presence of God and the presence of sin. Where sin existed, God could be approached only by the ritual of the temple. However, in the New Jerusalem sin is no longer a reality but is like a hideous nightmare, even locked out of the closet of memory. The actual presence of God with the redeemed eliminates the necessity for a temple, although the whole city may be thought of as a temple. Some have called attention to the fact that the New Jerusalem is the same shape as the Holy of Holies in the tabernacle and temple where God dwelt: a perfect cube. That is no accident, by the way. In the city of light God is present, and sin is absent; therefore, an edifice of a material substance is no longer necessary. The physical temple was a poor substitute for the presence of God. The New Jerusalem possesses the genuine article—God in person. It is probably the first place where God will make a personal appearance before man. What a glorious prospect this is!

The New Jerusalem will be independent of the sun and moon for light and life. What a contrast to the earth, which is utterly dependent upon the sun and the moon. It may be that the sun and moon will even be dependent upon the celestial city for power to transmit light, since the One who is the source of light and life will dwell within the city. Neither will light be furnished by the New Jerusalem Light and Power Company. The One who is light will be there, and the effulgence of His glory will be manifested in the New Jerusalem unhindered.

NEW CENTER OF THE NEW CREATION

And the nations of them which are saved shall walk in the light of it: and the kings of the earth do bring their glory and honour into it [Rev. 21:24].

And the nations shall walk amidst the light thereof: and the kings of the earth bring their glory into it.

"And the nations shall walk amidst the light thereof." It does not say they will live there, but that they will walk in the light of it. In other words, the New Jerusalem (instead of the sun and the moon) will give light unto the earth.

"And the kings of the earth bring their glory into it." This is my reason for saying that there will be a great deal of traffic commuting back and forth between the New Jerusalem and this earth down here. Not only will Israel come up there to worship, but the nations of the world which have entered eternity will also come up. It will not be their permanent abode, but they will come up there to worship. I believe that the church will be the priests at that time. We are told that we are a priesthood of believers.

And the gates of it shall not be shut at all by day: for there shall be no night there [Rev. 21:25].

And the gates thereof shall in no wise be shut by day (for there shall be no night there).

It is nonsense to say that the gates will not be shut at night because there is no night. Therefore, he says that they will not be shut by day. In other words, they are going to throw away the key because there will be no danger. In John's day, a walled city had gates for the purpose of protection. When the gate of a city was closed, it meant that an enemy was on the outside and that they were trying to keep him there.

And they shall bring the glory and honour of the nations into it.

And there shall in no wise enter into it any thing that defileth, neither whatsoever worketh abomination, or maketh a lie: but they which are written in the Lamb's book of life [Rev. 21:26–27].

And they shall bring the glory and the honor of the nations into it: and there shall in no wise enter into it anything unclean, or he that maketh an abomination and a lie: but only they that are written in the Lamb's book of life.

God has apparently accomplished His original purpose with man—fellowship. He now has a creature who is a free moral agent and who chooses to worship and serve Him eternally.

There can be no night, since the Lamb is the light, and He is eternally present.

The gates are not for protection, and they are never closed. Rather, they are the badge or coat of arms of the bride. Notice that these gates are of pearl. The pearl of great price has been purchased at a great price. In the parable (see Matt. 13:45–46) that the Lord Jesus gave, the pearl is not Christ whom the sinner buys. What is a sinner to pay for Christ?—he hasn't anything that he can pay. It is the other way around. The merchant man who bought that pearl was the Lord Jesus Christ, and the pearl is the bride. It is interesting that a pearl is formed by a grain of sand that gets into the body of a little oyster or mollusk of some kind, and that little marine creature begins to put around that grain a secretion that before long makes the pearl. The pearl of great price is *margarites* in the Greek, and if the church has a name, it is Margaret. The Lord Jesus Christ paid a great price to buy this pearl. This pearl was formed from His side. Someone has said, "I got into the heart of Christ through a spear wound." He was wounded for our transgressions; He was bruised for our iniquities. The church will be for the display of His grace throughout eternity to the absolute myriads of God's created intelligences. "That in the ages to come he might shew the exceeding riches of his grace in his kindness toward us through Christ Jesus" (Eph. 2:7).

In other words, in eternity you and I will be there on display. They will look at Vernon McGee and say: "Do you see that fellow? He deserved hell, and the Lord Jesus Christ died for him and paid a tremendous price. He trusted Christ; that is all he had to offer. Now look what the Lord Jesus has done for him. He has made him fit for heaven and made him acceptable in the beloved."

The church will be the fairest jewel of all when He makes up His jewels (see Mal. 3:17–18). When He makes up His jewels, the church is going to be on display. This is the reason that the New Jerusalem will be the center of the new heavens and the new earth.

The Lamb's Book of Life contains the names of the redeemed of all ages. No one who was not redeemed by the blood of Christ will ever be permitted to enter the portals of the New Jerusalem. There is a great gulf fixed between the saved and the lost.

The greatest joy that will capture the heart of the redeemed will be that of abiding in the presence of Christ for eternity. "That where I am, there ye may be also" is what He said in John 14:3. This is heaven, my friend, to be with Him. Revelation is all about Jesus Christ—He is the centerpiece of God's universe.

Our attention has already been directed to the fact that a redeemed remnant of Israel makes regular visits to the city of God. In verse 24 another group is identified who comes into the city to bring their glory and honor. These are the redeemed gentile nations which will occupy the earth together with Israel for eternity. These nations, like Israel, do not belong to the church, for they are redeemed after the church is removed from the earth (or before the church came into existence). They come as visitors to the city. They come as worshipers. In Hebrews 12:22 we are told there is also present an innumerable company of angels who evidently constitute the servant class. The city is cosmopolitan in character. All nationalities meet there, and the created intelligences of God walk the street of the New Jerusalem.

Among the multitudes, there is not one who will bring defilement or sin. How superior is this city to even the Garden of Eden where the lie of Satan made an entrance for sin. No lie or liar will ever enter the portals of the heavenly Jerusalem. All dwellers and all tourists are not only redeemed from sin but have also lost their taste for sin. They come through the gates which are never closed. The enjoyment of this glorious city is not restricted to the church, although they are the only ones who dwell there.

> Jerusalem, the golden, with milk and honey
>   blest!
>   Beneath thy contemplation sink heart and
>   voice oppressed;
> I know not, O I know not what joys await me
>   there;
>   What radiancy of glory, what bliss beyond
>   compare.
>   "Jerusalem the Golden"
>   —Bernard of Cluny

What a picture and how inadequately I have dealt with it. Oh, if only you and I both could be lifted up so that we might get a glimpse of the glory of that city and of the glory of the One who is its chief adornment, even the Lord Jesus Christ, and of the glorious prospect and privilege of being with Him throughout eternity. There is nothing to compare to it!

CHAPTER 22

THEME: River of the Water of Life, the Tree of Life; the promise of Christ's return; the final invitation

This chapter brings us to the final scenes of this great book of scenic wonders. It likewise brings us to the end of the Word of God. God gives us His final words here, and because they are last words, they have a greater significance. We are brought to the end of man's journey. The path has been rugged. Many questions remain unanswered, many problems remain unsolved, but man enters into eternity in fellowship again with God, and there all will be answered.

The Bible opens with God on the scene: "In the beginning God created the heaven and the earth" (Gen. 1:1). It concludes with Him on the scene and in full control of His own. He suffered, He paid a price, and He died—but the victory and the glory are His, and He is satisfied. Isaiah 53:11 puts it like this: "He shall see of the travail of his soul, and shall be satisfied: by his knowledge shall my righteous servant justify many; for he shall bear their iniquities."

RIVER OF THE WATER OF LIFE AND THE TREE OF LIFE

Chapter 22 opens with a beautiful description of the New Jerusalem.

And he shewed me a pure river of water of life, clear as crystal, proceeding out of the throne of God and of the Lamb.

In the midst of the street of it, and on either side of the river, was there the tree of life, which bare twelve manner of fruits, and yielded her fruit every month: and the leaves of the tree were for the healing of the nations [Rev. 22:1–2].

As usual I'll give my own literal translation of the Greek text throughout this chapter.

> *And he showed me a river of water of life, bright as crystal, proceeding out of the throne of God and of the Lamb. In the midst of the street thereof. And on this side of the river and on that was the tree of life, bearing twelve fruits, yielding its fruit every month: and the leaves of the tree were for the healing of the nations.*

Up to this chapter, the New Jerusalem seems to be all mineral and no vegetable. Its appearance is as the dazzling display of a fabulous jewelry store; we wonder if there is no soft grass to sit upon, no green trees to enjoy, and no water to drink or food to eat. However, here are introduced the elements which add a rich softness to this city of elaborate beauty.

There was a river in the first Eden which branched into four rivers. Although there was abundance of water, it is not called the water of life. Eden was a garden of trees among which was the Tree of Life. God kept the way open for man by the shedding of blood (see Gen. 3:24). In the New Jerusalem there is a river of the Water of Life, and the throne of God is its living fountain supplying an abundance of water.

"The tree of life" is a fruit tree, bearing twelve kinds of fruits each month. There is a continuous supply in abundance and variety. In eternity man *will* eat and drink. That is a great relief to many of us, I am sure. The menu is varied but is restricted to fruits, as it was in the Garden of Eden: "And God said, Behold, I have given you every herb bearing seed, which is upon the face of all the earth, and every tree, in the which is the fruit of a tree yielding seed; to you it shall be for meat. And to every beast of the earth, and to every fowl of the air, and to every thing that creepeth upon the earth, wherein there is life, I have given every green herb for meat: and it was so" (Gen. 1:29–30).

There is a tendency to spiritualize this passage in Revelation and compare it to the fruit of the Spirit. I have no objection to that and would rather take that viewpoint myself, provided we hold to the literal interpretation, which I think you can do through this section.

Although it does seem highly symbolic, I think we are dealing with that which is quite literal, for we are still talking about heaven.

Even the leaves of the tree are beneficial—they have a medicinal value. Why healing is needed in a perfect universe is a very good question and a difficult problem to solve. Perhaps it is a sort of first-aid kit which demonstrates the old adage, "An ounce of prevention is worth a pound of cure." I personally believe that the bodies of the earth dwellers in eternity will be different from the bodies of the believers in the church who are to be like Christ (that is, their bodies will be like His). The bodies of the earth dwellers may need renewing from time to time. This may be the reason that they come up to the New Jerusalem—not only to worship, but also to be renewed physically and spiritually. At least the prevention is there.

However, the possibility of sin entering simply is not there.

And there shall be no more curse: but the throne of God and of the Lamb shall be in it; and his servants shall serve him:

And they shall see his face; and his name shall be in their foreheads.

And there shall be no night there; and they need no candle, neither light of the sun; for the Lord God giveth them light: and they shall reign for ever and ever [Rev. 22:3-5].

And there shall be no curse anymore: and the throne of God and of the Lamb shall be therein: and His servants shall do Him service: and they shall see His face; and His name shall be on their foreheads. And there shall be night no more; and they need no light of lamp, neither light of sun; for the Lord God shall give them light: and they shall reign for ever and ever.

The first creation was blighted by the curse of sin, and this old earth on which you and I live today bears many scar marks of the curse of sin. The new creation will never be marred by sin. Sin will never be permitted to enter even potentially. It was potentially in the Garden of Eden in the tree of the knowledge of good and evil. The very presence of God and the Lamb will be adequate to prevent it. It was during the absence of God in the Garden of Eden that the tempter came to our first parents.

The throne of God and the Lamb are in the New Jerusalem. It is general headquarters for God the Father and God the Son. The notable absence of any reference to the Holy Spirit does need some explanation. You see, in the first creation the Holy Spirit came to renovate and renew the blighted earth: "The Spirit of God brooded over the face of the waters" (see Gen. 1:2). He is the instrument today of regeneration in the hearts and lives of sinners. There will be no need of His work in the new creation in this connection; therefore the silence of God at this point is eloquent.

"His servants shall do Him service" reveals that heaven is not a place of unoccupied idleness but a place of ceaseless activity. It will not be necessary to rest in order to give the body an opportunity to recuperate. The word for "service" is a peculiar one. In his *Word Studies in the New Testament* Dr. Vincent says, "It came to be used by the Jews in a very special sense, to denote the service rendered to Jehovah by the Israelites as His peculiar people." We read this in the Epistle to the Hebrews: "Then verily the first covenant had also ordinances of divine service, and a worldly sanctuary. . . . Now when these things were thus ordained, the priests went always into the first tabernacle, accomplishing the service of God" (Heb. 9:1, 6). It will be a peculiar service to God that you and I will perform in eternity. What it is, I do not know. He may give us charge of universes. There will be ceaseless activity since there is no night. Man will at last fulfill his destiny and satisfy the desires of his heart.

Man will at last see His face. This was the supreme desire voiced by Moses in the Old Testament and Philip in the New Testament. It is the highest objective for living. What divine satisfaction!

"His name shall be in their foreheads." Each person will bear the name of Christ. Each will be like Him, yet without disturbing his own peculiar personality. I have always said this facetiously, but it could be true: If He will, I want God to let me teach the Bible in heaven. I want to attend the classes which Paul teaches, and then I would like to teach those people who were members of the churches I served on the earth but who would not attend the midweek Bible studies. I have asked to teach them for one million years and, I tell you, they won't think it is heaven for that first million years! I am really going to work them and make them catch up. Whether that will be true or not, I don't know, but I do say that we are all going to be busy there.

Our attention in this section is called to the direct lighting of the new creation. There will be no light holders such as the sun or light reflectors such as the moon. God lights the universe by His presence, for God is light.

It is in eternity that the bride will reign with Christ. Who knows but what He will give to each saint a world or a solar system or a galactic system to operate. Remember that Adam was given dominion over the old creation on this earth.

PROMISE OF THE RETURN OF CHRIST

And he said unto me, These sayings are faithful and true: and the Lord God of the holy prophets sent his angel to shew unto his servants the things which must shortly be done.

Behold, I come quickly: blessed is he that keepeth the sayings of the prophecy of this book [Rev. 22:6–7].

And he said unto me, These words are faithful and true: and the Lord, the God of the spirits of the prophets, sent His angel to show unto His servants the things which must shortly come to pass. And behold, I come quickly. Blessed is he that keepeth the words of the prophecy of this book.

The important thing to note is that when He says, "And behold, I come quickly," He means *rapidly*. This is repeated again in verse 12 and verse 20. It is repeated three times here at the end: "Behold, I come quickly"—not *shortly* or *immediately* or even *soon*. These events that we have been looking at in Revelation, beginning with chapter 4, take place in a period of not more than seven years, and most of them are confined to the last three and one-half years. The encouragement here is that the Lord Jesus says that it will not be a long period: "I am coming shortly. I will soon be there." But that means *when* we get to this period. We are not exactly accurate when we speak of "the soon coming of Christ." I have said that many times myself, but I do not think it is an accurate term, and it gives the wrong impression.

The Lord Jesus puts His own seal upon this book: "These words are faithful and true" means that no man is to trifle with them by spiritualizing them or reducing them to meaningless symbols. Our Lord is talking about reality. At the beginning of this book, there was a blessing pronounced upon those who read and hear and keep these words. In conclusion, the Lord Jesus repeats the blessing upon those who keep these words. This is a book not to merely satisfy the curiosity of the natural man but to live and act upon.

And I John saw these things, and heard them. And when I had heard and seen, I fell down to worship before the feet of the angel which shewed me these things.

Then saith he unto me, See thou do it not: for I am thy fellow-servant, and of thy brethren the prophets, and of them which keep the sayings of this book: worship God.

And he saith unto me, Seal not the sayings of the prophecy of this book: for the time is at hand.

He that is unjust, let him be unjust still: and he which is filthy, let him be filthy still: and he that is righteous, let him be righteous still: and he that is holy, let him be holy still [Rev. 22:8–11].

And I John am he that heard and saw these things. And when I heard and saw, I fell down to worship before the feet of the angel that showed me these things. And he

*saith unto me, See (thou do it) not: I am a fellow servant
with thee and with thy brethren the prophets, and with
them that keep the words of this book: worship God. And
he saith unto me, Seal not up the words of the prophecy
of this book; for the time is at hand. He that is unrighteous, let him do unrighteousness still; and he that is
filthy, let him be made filthy still: and he that is righteous, let him do righteousness still: and he that is holy
let him be made holy still.*

Notice John's final and oft-repeated statement that he was both auditor
and spectator to the scenes in this book. This is the method that was
put down at the very opening of the book. It is the first television program, for John both saw and heard.

John was so impressed that his natural reaction was to fall down
and worship the angel. The simplicity and meekness of the angel are
impressive. Though the angels were created above man, this angel
identifies himself as a fellow servant with John and the other
prophets. He was merely a messenger to communicate God's Word to
man, and he directs all worship to God. Christ is the centerpiece of
the Book of Revelation—don't lose sight of Him.

"Seal not up the words of the prophecy of this book." Daniel was
told to seal up the words of his prophecy because of the long interval
before the fulfillment of it (see Dan. 12:4). In fact, we in the twentieth
century have not come to the Seventieth Week of Daniel yet. In contrast, the prophecy given to John was even then in process of being
fulfilled. For nineteen hundred years, the church has been passing
through the time periods of the seven churches given in chapters 2—3.

"He that is unrighteous . . . he that is filthy"—probably the most
frightful condition of the lost is revealed here, even more so than at the
Great White Throne judgment of chapter 20. The sinful condition of
the lost is a permanent and eternal thing, although it is not static, for
the suggestion is that the unrighteous will increasingly become more
unrighteous: "he that is filthy, let him be made filthy still." The condition of the lost gets worse until each becomes a monster of sin. This
thought is frightful!

On the other hand, neither is the condition of the servant of God static. They will continue to grow in righteousness and holiness. Heaven is not static. Even in the Millennium "of the increase of His kingdom there shall be no end." What a glorious and engaging prospect this should be for the child of God! We shall have all eternity to grow in knowledge.

And, behold, I come quickly; and my reward is with me, to give every man according as his work shall be.

I am Alpha and Omega, the beginning and the end, the first and the last.

Blessed are they that do his commandments, that they may have right to the tree of life, and may enter in through the gates into the city.

For without are dogs, and sorcerers, and whoremongers, and murderers, and idolators, and whosoever loveth and maketh a lie.

I Jesus have sent mine angel to testify unto you these things in the churches. I am the root and the offspring of David, and the bright and morning star [Rev. 22:12–16].

Behold, I come quickly; and my reward is with me, to render to each man according as his work is. I am the Alpha and the Omega, the first and the last, the beginning and the end. Blessed are they that wash their robes, in order that theirs shall be authority over the tree of life, and may enter by the gates into the city. Without are the dogs, and the sorcerers, and the fornicators, and the murderers, and the idolators, and every one that loveth and maketh a lie. I Jesus have sent mine angel to testify unto you these things for the churches. I am the root and the offspring of David, the bright, the morning star.

The church should know this program of God. Either the angel is bearing a very personal word from Jesus, or else the Lord is breaking through and saying it personally. Our Lord promises that He is coming again. That is His personal declaration. No believer can doubt or deny this all-important and personal promise of the Lord Jesus.

He will personally reward each believer individually—those in the church at the Rapture as well as those of Israel and the Gentiles at His return to set up His Kingdom at the Millennium.

It is little wonder that Paul could write: "That I may know him, and the power of his resurrection, and the fellowship of his sufferings, being made conformable unto his death; if by any means I might attain unto the resurrection of the dead. Not as though I had already attained, either were already perfect: but I follow after, if that I may apprehend that for which also I am apprehended of Christ Jesus. Brethren, I count not myself to have apprehended: but this one thing I do, forgetting those things which are behind, and reaching forth unto those things which are before, I press toward the mark for the prize of the high calling of God in Christ Jesus" (Phil. 3:10–14).

Again the Lord Jesus asserts His deity: "I am the Alpha and the Omega, the first and the last, the beginning and the end." He said this at the beginning of Revelation, and He concludes with it.

Only blood-washed believers have authority over the Tree of Life and access to the Holy City (see Eph. 1:7–12).

"Dogs" come off rather badly in Scripture. This perhaps does not mean that there will be no dogs in heaven, but because dogs were scavengers in the ancient world they were considered unclean and impure. Also, "dogs" was the designation for Gentiles (see Matt. 15:21–28) and Paul's label for Judaizers (see Phil. 3:2).

Apparently the Lord Jesus had sent His angel with this very personal message. "I Jesus"—He takes the name of His saviorhood, the name He received when He took upon Himself humanity, and the name that no man knows but He Himself. You and I are going to spend eternity just centering on Him and His person. My friend, if you are not interested in Jesus today, I do not know why you would want to go to heaven. That is all we are going to talk about up there; we are going to talk about Him.

He is called "the root and the offspring of David," which connects Him with the Old Testament. But He is "the bright and morning star" to the church. Have you noticed that the bright and morning star always appears at the darkest time of the night? Its appearance indicates that the sun will be coming up shortly. The Old Testament ended with the promise that "the Sun of righteousness will arise with healing in his wings"—that is the Old Testament hope (see Mal. 4:2). But to us, He is the Bright and Morning Star who will come at a very dark moment.

FINAL INVITATION AND WARNING

And the Spirit and the bride say, Come. And let him that heareth say, Come. And let him that is athirst come. And whosoever will, let him take the water of life freely.

For I testify unto every man that heareth the words of the prophecy of this book, If any man shall add unto these things, God shall add unto him the plagues that are written in this book:

And if any man shall take away from the words of the book of this prophecy, God shall take away his part out of the book of life, and out of the holy city, and from the things which are written in this book [Rev. 22:17–19].

And the Spirit and the bride say, Come. And he that heareth, let him say, Come. And he that is athirst, let him come: he that will, let him take the water of life freely. I testify unto every man that heareth the words of the prophecy of this book, If any man shall add unto them, God shall add the plagues which are written in this book: and if any man shall take away from the words of the book of this prophecy, God shall take away his part from the tree of life, and out of the holy city, which are written in this book.

The bride is the church. This is a twofold invitation—an invitation to Christ to come and an invitation to sinners to come to Christ before He returns. The Holy Spirit is in the world today, and He joins in the prayer of the church which says, "Lord Jesus, come, come."

The Holy Spirit is performing His work in the world today in converting and convicting men. He works through the Word and through the church which proclaims His Word. The invitation to men is to come and to take the Water of Life: "Ho, every one that thirsteth, come ye to the waters . . . without money and without price" (Isa. 55:1). The Lord Jesus stood and said, ". . . If any man thirst, let him come unto me, and drink" (John 7:37). That is the invitation that goes out today. If you are tired of drinking at the cesspools of this world, He invites you to come. What an invitation this is to come to Him!

FINAL PROMISE AND PRAYER

He which testifieth these things saith, Surely I come quickly. Amen. Even so, come, Lord Jesus.

The grace of our Lord Jesus Christ be with you all. Amen [Rev. 22:20–21].

He who testifieth these things saith, Yes: I come quickly. Amen: Come, Lord Jesus. The grace of the Lord Jesus be with all the saints. Amen.

"Yea: I come quickly"—not *soon*, but when these things begin to come to pass, He is even then at the door.

"Come, Lord Jesus" is the heart cry of every true believer.

"The grace of our Lord Jesus Christ be with you all. Amen." The Old Testament ends with a curse; the New Testament ends with a benediction of grace upon the believers. Grace is offered to all, but if any man (regardless of his merit) refuses the offer which is extended, he must bear the judgment pronounced in this book.

Grace is still offered to man. It is God's method of saving sinners.

Amazing grace! how sweet the sound,
That saved a wretch like me!
I once was lost, but now am found,
Was blind, but now I see.
—John Newton

BIBLIOGRAPHY

(Recommended for Further Study)

Barnhouse, Donald Grey. *Revelation, an Expository Commentary*. Grand Rapids, Michigan: Zondervan Publishing House, 1971.

Criswell, W. A. *Expository Sermons on Revelation*. Grand Rapids, Michigan: Zondervan Publishing House, 1966.

Epp, Theodore H. *Practical Studies in Revelation*. Lincoln, Nebraska: Back to the Bible Broadcast, 1969.

Gaebelein, Arno C. *The Revelation*. Neptune, New Jersey: Loizeaux Brothers, 1915.

Hoyt, Herman A. *The Revelation of the Lord Jesus Christ*. Winona Lake, Indiana: Brethren Missionary Herald, 1966.

Ironside, H. A. *Lectures on the Book of Revelation*. Neptune, New Jersey: Loizeaux Brothers, 1960. (Especially good for young converts.)

Larkin, Clarence. *The Book of Revelation*. Philadelphia, Pennsylvania: Published by the author, 1919. (Includes fine charts.)

Lindsey, Hal. *There's a New World Coming*. Santa Ana, California: Vision House Publishers, 1973.

McGee, J. Vernon. *Reveling Through Revelation*. 2 vols. Pasadena, California: Thru the Bible Books, 1962.

Newell, William R. *The Book of Revelation*. Chicago, Illinois: Moody Press, 1935.

Phillips, John. *Exploring Revelation*. Chicago, Illinois: Moody Press, 1974.

Ryrie, Charles C. *Revelation*. Chicago, Illinois: Moody Press, 1968. (A fine, inexpensive survey.)

BIBLIOGRAPHY

Scott, Walter. *Exposition of the Revelation of Jesus Christ*. London: Pickering and Inglis, n.d.

Seiss, J. A. *The Apocalypse, Lectures on the Book of Revelation*. Grand Rapids, Michigan: Zondervan Publishing House, 1957.

Smith, J. B. *A Revelation of Jesus Christ*. Scottsdale, Pennsylvania: Herald Press, 1961.

Strauss, Lehman. *The Book of Revelation*. Neptune, New Jersey: Loizeaux Brothers, 1964.

Walvoord, John F. *The Revelation of Jesus Christ*. Chicago, Illinois: Moody Press, 1966. (Excellent comprehensive treatment.)